DRIVING

GUIDE

TO GET TO HEAVEN

Written By: Dr. Raymond Saintil

ARPress
ILLUMINATING IDEAS
EMPOWERING VOICES

ARPress
45 Dan Road Suite 5
Canton MA 02021
Hotline: 1(888) 821-0229
Fax: 1(508) 545-7580

Ordering Information:
Quantity sales. Special discounts are available on quantity purchases by corporations, associations, and others. For details, contact the publisher at the address above.

Printed in the United States of America.

ISBN-13:   Softcover   979-8-89389-881-1
                eBook   979-8-89389-882-8

Library of Congress Control Number: 2024923867

Table of Content

DEDICATION

To be written…

FOREWORD

I have engaged in writing for the 2nd time. I hope that this bookwill please all those who read it and that it will help them in their Christian, marital, social and political lives.

PREFACE

This book is written under the guidance of the Almighty, and it aims to build a sound marriage, according to the Lord. Building a sound marriage is a daily decision. Be committed to resolving disputes quickly. "Everything is vanity," said the writer of the book of Ecclesiastes. Do not destroy yourself with evil words, but on the contrary, speak words of life for each other, words that bring peace, words that communicate grace and edify, words that promote and encourage your spouse. Be committed to your spouse's success because you will benefit from it. Your support will build the intimacy and fulfillment of your relationship. Because unity and harmony are the main ingredients of a successful marriage. The three (3) key areas that must bring a particular Christian couple together are: mutual love, love for God, and love for his church. May God bless you and renew while you're struggling in this incomprehensible world.

APPRECIATIONS

I would like to thank the Great Architect of the Universe who, through his powerful hand, allowed me to write this book for the first time. Honestly, i could never have accomplished this dream without the presence of God's holy spirit. I dedicate this book in particular: To my respectful wife, Bernadette Saintil, for her spiritual and moral support throughout the writing; To my three sons Rosando Labajola Saintil, Raygivenson Saintil, his wife Shequina Glorie Saintil, their two children, Layla Saintil, Raygivenson Saintil Junior, Markcampbell Saintil , To my nephew Patrick Pierre, an American Law enforcement of immigration officer with a degree in agronomy from Mexico, and his wife Emmanuela Pierre: To our friend Sabine Jean Baptiste; To Sister Viola Marcelin. A big thank you also to my parents who invested their money and efforts to get me through high school and university. Unfortunately, they are no longer with us today. I also dedicate this book to pastors from all over the world, as well as to all readers, not to mention professors from all universities and theological schools.

CHAPTER 1
INTRODUCTION -
ANALOGY –

Outcomes for the Christian home. Making disciples, the most neglected order of Jesus Christ. All over the world, thousands of people have become Christians, having accepted Jesus Christ as their personal savior, and have been baptized by immersion according to biblical teaching. But Jesus' order is precise: Make disciples and not only converts, members, sympathizers. This is the most neglected order of Jesus in the present Church.

Is not one of the recurring problems of the Church that many Christians, after years of conversion, are still babies in Christ? They were born again, but never grew in maturity in their faith and never became true disciples of Jesus. In addition, many of them sometimes shame the name of Christ and his Church.

THE FAMILY'S HOPE

How to raise your children according to the Lord?

King Ahab ruled his kingdom outside the will of God. His son, King Asarias, did the same thing as his father. According to Proverbs 13:24, we should not neglect raising our children with rods. And he who does not punish his children, does not love them.

According to Proverbs 19:18, he who spares his rod hates his son, but he who loves him seeks to correct him.

THE CHRISTIAN'S HOME

Knowing how to manage money and property is not the only important requirement for being a worker or servant of God. The apostle Paul tells us that one of the fundamental requirements of a Church leader, and even an assistant, is to be also a good household caretaker.

In fact, his argument is very simple: if a man does not know how to run his own house, how can he take care of God's Church (I Timothy 3:5)? Here, Paul naturally refers to the action of leading or managing his home according to God's instructions. Whether you are a servant of God or a simple believer, you need to be the steward of your home. And i wrote this to help you meet that need.

Through the study of this book, you will learn to manage your home and use your house according to God's will. In fact, you will also be able to share this teaching in your church or community.

THE CHRISTIAN HOUSEHOLD

PHOTO

The Christian household is a place where the Lord's presence can be felt, a haven for guests, a testimony for the locality.

OBJECTIVES OF THIS BOOK

After reading this book, you should be able to describe the duties of each member of the Christian family, including stewardship, and you will realize the importance of stewardship of your home.

You will only have to name several ways to use your home for God's glory.

A RESPONSIBLE CHRISTIAN

As you carefully study this strategy, ask the Lord to help you so that these truths become an integral part of your life. You may discover some principles that you can start implementing now!

Keywords

Abnormal
Arbitrary
Authority
Dedication
Editorial - oasis Founder- source haven-symbol integrity
Strategy development of this manual.

THE CHRISTIAN FAMILY - ITS FOUNDER

Objective:

Identify the reason why God is the founder and owner of the family.

God is the founder of the family. He established it when he created man and woman (Genesis 1:28). As the founder of the family, God has property rights over it. It is his family and he is therefore the owner.

a)   1- God is the founder and owner of the family because he:
        a) Knew that man would sin.
        (b) Is the creator of the family.
        c) Ordered the family to obey.

OUR HOMES

Its Model Objective 2

Describe the model that the Christian family should follow.

Christian household is a family whose members live together according to the model established by God. Read 1 Corinthians 11:3, Ephesians 5:2 and Ephesians 6:4 to see the divine principles of authority and relationship that are part of this model. Here we see Christ as the head of the husband and the husband as the head of the family.

Children are under the authority of their parents. In other words, each family member is subject to the respective authorities that God has placed at its head... These different relationships can be illustrated as follows:

- Christ
- Husband
- Wife
- Children

In addition, these verses also show how this authority should function within the family. The model is the relationship between Christ and His Church. This is the example of Christ's authority, direction and love that must be followed by those who exercise authority in the family. Christ was never a dictatorial leader.

He always guided his disciples by giving directions and giving them in love, offering his life as an example. Above all else, Christ must be recognized as the supreme authority by all family members. Indeed, it is only under this condition that the family can function as God intended it to function.

It would be absolutely impossible to imagine a real Christian family without Christ at its head.

THE DUTIES OF ITS MEMBERS

Objective 3

Identify statements about relationships between family members that are consistent with what the Bible teaches. For a family to function according to God's plan, each member of the family should fulfill his or her respective duties.

MARRIED COUPLES

In order to be able to make plans for the family, God chose to unite a man and a woman to become a couple. God says: "It is not good for man to be alone; I will give him a help that will be his counterpart (Genesis 2:18)". God formed the woman from the body of the man and then declared that man and woman would again be one body through marriage (Genesis 2:24)! What a profound mystery all this is (Ephesians 5:32-33)!

In order to preserve this unity, God has established certain rules that both partners should follow in an identical way. These rules are as follows:

Don't deprive each other. This is exactly what the apostle Paul says in 1 Corinthians 7:3-5 with reference to marital relationships. Does that surprise you? If the Bible has much to say about the misuse of sex, this Bible passage is the only one that teaches its correct use. Of course, this use of sexual relations is limited to the sphere of marriage. Marriage begins with the physical union of the couple (Genesis 2:24). It is therefore natural that the Scriptures prescribe a standard for the continuity of this union. According to this standard, each partner should satisfy the physical needs of the other because they no longer own their own bodies. Each of them belongs to the other. If the couple obeys this principle and follows the resulting norm, their marriage will be happier and infidelity will be greatly discouraged.

1-Read 1 Corinthians 7:3-5 and answer the following questions: A-When is the only time when partners, united by marriage, should refrain from sexual relations with each other?

B-What is the condition that must first be met?

The Bible teaches us: be faithful to each other. When a man and a woman are united by the bonds of marriage in the Lord, they promise each other mutual fidelity. God wants these promises to be honored in their married life.

In other words, both men and women should remember that their bodies belong first to the Lord and then to their partners.

The apostle Paul declares that if a believer unites his body with that of a prostitute, he actually takes a part of the body of Christ and makes it a part of the body of the prostitute!

The believer's body is indeed a part or member of the body of Christ (1 Corinthians 6:14-17). Similarly, if a husband or wife unites his or her body with another person, they unite their spouse's body with that person's body! Because their bodies belong to their spouses and each body is one with the other.

Infidelity is therefore an abnormality; it is the union of a member of the body that is the couple with the body of a stranger. Knowing this, it is therefore not strange that infidelity brings with it so much distress in marriage.

The Lord God speaks harshly of separation. The Bible, the word of God, says: Do not separate what God has united. Jesus said that from the moment a man and a woman unite as husband and wife, they no longer form two distinct entities because God has united them (Matthew 19:6). They are one! In the light of this, divorce also becomes a distortion, a human interference in God's affairs.

Partners should not divorce because they have no right to separate what God has united. Although divorce was allowed in the Old Testament, we should not forget, Jesus told us, that this permission existed only because men were so difficult to teach (Matthew 19:8). The norm established by God at the beginning was never abolished. That's why he says: Love each other.

The idea that a man and a woman marry because of romantic love has been widely adopted in the modern world. Love is considered a mutual attraction between a man and a woman. When this attraction ceases to exist, it seems reasonable and in good taste to break up this marriage. Yet, the biblical idea of love, according to the Scriptures, commands the couple to love each other (Ephesians 5:25, Titus 2:4). If a couple thinks that their marriage is destroyed for lack of mutual love, it is time for the spouses to begin to love each other, that is, to obey the precepts of the Lord.

What is the biblical idea of love? It is certainly not a pure and simple physical and emotional attraction. There is a lot of personal satisfaction in this type of love. On the contrary, the love that the Bible teaches is a love that is given, that is offered. Each partner thinks about what he can give to the other. This is the kind of love that the apostle Paul teaches in 1 Corinthians 13:4-7. This is the kind of love that can keep the wedding boat afloat in the midst of life's raging waters.

DEDICATE YOURSELF TO EACH OTHER

Dedication is essential to Christian marriage. This commitment includes each other's dedication to each other and the willingness to place God at the centre of your relationship. This is the best way to find a solution to the problems of mutual understanding and relationships that afflict us at one point or another in our common life. There can be no basis for marital harmony and stability if the basis of marriage does not include dedication.

OUR HOMES

The best method given by the Gospel is Christ's devotion to his sheep. This is a good example of the endurance quality of this kind of dedication (John 13:1).

Now let's talk about our homes.

Mutual respect, an excellent medicine for homes, according to the word of God.

Respect each other.

The spouses should respect each other, one in relation to the other, even if it seems to one another that the other does not deserve it and vice versa (Ephesians 5:33; 1 Peter 3:7). They should have great consideration for each other, for to decry each other while being united and forming one flesh would be to decry oneself. The woman should respect her husband because he is the authority that God has placed over her; the husband, on the other hand, should respect his wife because she is the appropriate companion that God has given her and the one who will receive with him the grace of God's life (1 Peter 3:7).

Now, we're going to do a little exercise. Please circle the letter in front of each statement that is true, as the Bible teaches about married couples.

A - Couples who no longer love each other should not try to continue their marriage.

B - A wife (or husband) should not refuse to meet the sexual needs of her (or his) partner.

C - Divorce is mainly bad because children are generally affected by it.

WOMEN/WIVES

The word of God indicates two duties specific to Christian women. The Bible is formal: Women, be submissive to your husbands.

In ancient times, women were slaves to their husbands. But among the Israelites, she had a better status. However, it is in Christ that the woman was able to regain her true dignity: "There is neither woman nor man, for you are one in Jesus Christ (Galatians 3:28)."

However, within marriage, God has given a specific model of relationships, responsibilities and authority. Ephesians 5:22-33 shows us the respective roles of man and woman. While God has given man the responsibility of directing and directing the home, he has prescribed the duty of the woman to submit to this direction and authority, in the same way that the Church submits to the direction of Christ (according to Ephesians 5:22 and 24; Colossians 3:18 and Titus 2:5; 1Peter 3:1-5).

CHAPTER 2
THE MIRROR

The Bible is the mirror of all those who want to go to heaven (According to Matthew, chapter 7: 13-14).It is the door and the path that lead to life. It is clear that we are in a spiritual warfare, or a spiritual warfare. Life has its ups and downs. The road of life, dear friends, dear brothers and sisters, is slippery, with curves and precipices. When the path is spacious, many enter it; but when it is narrow, very few people use it. Satan the Devil, man's fierce enemy, said: "I will shape for you the great spacious road, the I-95, the one called in French the highway. Satan, man's enemy, said to him: Why do you take the narrow road, the one that takes so long to get you to your destination? Why don't you want to go by the spacious road For example, consider the case of Haiti's narrow and dangerous roads. Going south, before arriving at Miragoane, the presence of many curves, especially as we approach Morne Tapion, makes the road very dangerous.

Similarly, in the south-east, around the city of Jacmel, there is a hill called Chen pap jwenn (The dog will not find). With its many towers, detours and precipices, the road is difficult to access, and many passengers died, including pastors on a mission.

The Israeli people walked for 40 years to reach Canaan. This is a journey that could have taken only two (2) months. But the Lord saw fit to lead his people through the longest way. Do you know how many Israelites have arrived at their destination? Only two that the Bible calls two heroes: Caleb and Joshua. Moses, number one, was not so lucky. He had almost reached his goal, but the Lord said to him: "My dear

Moses, you have made a great effort to reach this place, but look at Canaan, you cannot enter it.

David was also in a curve. Looking down, he saw a beautiful and beautiful woman and asked who owned her. She was told that she was Ury's wife. David, the Bible teaches us, considered that Ury did not deserve such a woman and decided to kill him. So he sent him to war, leading a troop, where Ury was fatally wounded in the chest.

Ury's pretty widow became David's wife and found herself pregnant with his works. Thus David was able to successfully cross the murderer curve and the adultery curve. We should therefore take great care on the spacious roads of life (according to Romans 7:11, destructive sin)

THE CRY OF VICTORY AND REWARDS

THE LAST ENEMY TO BE DESTROYED IS DEATH.

The most cruel death has made people cry in this perverse world because of the anxiety we live in.

The architect of the universe, the great Jesus par excellence, has power over death. To win, you must work in the battlefield. Paul had to say: I fought the good fight of the faith, I finished my race, now the crown of justice is reserved for me. Paul resolved that he had worked well and that his work had been approved by the chief for whom he was working. That is why he was able to shout out: O death, where is your victory? O death, where is your sting?

The sting of death is sin; and the power of sin is the law. Paul goes on to say: but thanks be to God, who gives us victory through our Lord Jesus Christ! So my beloved brothers, be firm, unshakeable, always progress in the work of the Lord, knowing that your work will not be in vain in the Lord. The opposite of progress is loss or regression. Why does Paul talk like that? This is because the resurrection of Christ is our guarantee.

Paul continues his speech: I remind you, Brothers, of the Gospel that I have preached to you, that you have received, in which you stand firm, and by which you are also saved, if you keep it in the terms in which I preached it to you; otherwise you would have believed in vain. I have transmitted to you, above all, what I had received: Christ died for our sins, according to the Scriptures; he was buried, he rose again on the third (3rd) day, and was seen by Cephas, then by the twelve (1 Corinthians 15:26-58; 1 Corinthians 15:26).

El ultimo enemigo que sera destruido es la muerte . (The last enemy to be destroyed is death.). 1 Corinthians 15:26 - The last enemy to be destroyed is death .1 Peter 3: 1-5 According to the scriptures, it is difficult for some women to understand what it means to be submissive. They believe that there should be full equality between men and women in all areas of life. But this way of thinking is not realistic because of the multiple differences between men and women. While it is true that everyone has the same spiritual rights and responsibilities before God, it is also true that people who have the same rights freely choose the leaders to whom they submit. By the act of marriage, the woman therefore freely chooses to become a member of the household and to submit to the authority that is included in the model established by God for the household. God never intended that man and woman should be rivals for each other, but rather that they should complement each other (according to 1 Corinthians 11:11-12). When this is well understood and applied, happiness and harmony can exist.

BE GOOD HOUSEWIVES

That being said, taking care of the house is one of the other obligations that God has entrusted to women (according to Titus 2:5). You can notice the magnificent praise that this kind of woman receives in Proverbs 31:10-31. Suppose, for example, that a woman asks you this question: "Why should I submit to my husband, when Galatians 3:28 says that there is no longer any difference between man and woman? On your side, what will be your answer?

ABOUT HUSBANDS, WHAT DO THEY SAY?

God has given the husband a primary obligation: To love his wife (according to Ephesians 5:25; Colossians 3:19). In the light of the Bible, let us now examine the characteristics of this love. According to the Scriptures, the husband's love for his wife is considered a love that is given. The husband is even willing to sacrifice his life for his wife, as Christ did for the Church, because of his immense love for her (according to Ephesians 5:25). We can say that it is a courageous love, a love that has reached its most complete expression

THE LOVE OF THE HUSBAND FOR HIS WIFE

The husband's love for his wife is a love of himself. This would seem to contradict the previous statement, and yet this is exactly what the Bible says: "He who loves his wife loves himself (according to Ephesians 5:28)". He does not love someone else, as a man who loves his neighbor does, but he loves himself. He loves his wife as he provides for her physical, emotional, spiritual needs and takes care of her in the same way that he takes care of himself, because the two are really one flesh (according to Ephesians 5:29). He is considerate of his wife's needs and problems, just as Christ is to those of the Church. Through this attitude, it acts in the way Christ treats the Church, which is his body.

The husband's love for his wife is a love full of sweetness. The husband does not treat his wife harshly (according to Colossians 3:19), but gently, acknowledging his weakness (according to 1 Peter 3:7). He leads her by showing her love and tenderness. A husband who loves his wife with such love should have no difficulty in obtaining his submission. In other words, a woman who has a husband who loves him in this way should have no problem submitting to him.

We want to do a little exercise to see if you understand what the word of God has just said. Next to each statement below, write True or False, as appropriate. Then quote at least one Bible verse to support each of your answers.

1- When a husband loves his wife, he actually loves himself.

2- The main obligation that God has given to husbands is to tell their wives what to do.

3- Since the husband's love for his wife is a love that is gives, it cannot be both a love of oneself.

There is a remark that the Bible, the word of God, places before the woman, the obligation to submit to her husband; and before the husband, the obligation to love his wife. It is very important that each partner takes on its own responsibilities and does not try to force or force the other to carry out his or her own.

The husband cannot and should not try to force his wife to submit to him. That's not possible! On the other hand, the wife cannot force her husband to love her.

According to the Scriptures, each person must take on his own responsibility and let the other do the same. Otherwise, a woman may refuse to submit to her husband until he shows her love, or the husband may refuse to love his wife until she submits to him. This is a situation of you first of all that prevents each of the spouses from accomplishing God's model.

THE DUTY/DUTIES OF CHILDREN

What is the duty of children? According to God's commandment, the duty of children is to obey their parents (according to Ephesians 6:1-3; Colossians 3:20). The authority of parents is based on God's authority because they represent him in the household. The Scriptures mentioned above give us four main reasons why children should be obedient.

1-Observance is a Christian duty

2- Obedience is the right thing to do

3-Observance is pleasing to God.

4- There is a promise of success and long life for those who respect their parents. Christ himself is the most superb example of obedience. He obeyed his heavenly father (according to Philippians 2:8) as well as his earthly parents (according to Luke 2:51).

CHAPTER 3
THE DUTY OF PARENTS

God has entrusted parents with the task of instructing, disciplining and loving their children (according to Ephesians, chapter 6:4 and Titus 2:4).

TEACH YOUR CHILDREN

Parents have a duty to teach their children everything about their present and future lives (according to Proverbs 22:6). The parents' teaching should include: A) The Word of God (from Deuteronomy 6:7). This is the foundation of your teaching.

B) Obedience (according to Genesis 18:19). Children will learn the principle of authority and thus grow up as law-abiding citizens.

C) Work. You will help them in this way not to be lazy or to become delinquents.

D) Stewardship. This will allow them to become people responsible before God and men.

THE EFFECTIVENESS OF TEACHING

For teaching to be effective, it must be put into practice. One of the forms of this implementation is to establish rules that children must obey. But be careful! Do not establish rules that you yourself are not able to observe (from Romans 2:21-22). Your teaching should be accompanied by your example. If you do not do this, you will confuse and irritate your children (according to Colossians 3:21).

DISCIPLINE YOUR CHILDREN

If children do not obey the rules set by their parents, they should be disciplined (according to Proverbs 19:18; and 29:17). Let us now talk about the correction of children.

Correction is a demonstration of love for children (according to Proverbs 13:24). On the other hand, lack of discipline is the evidence that parents do not love their children.

THE USE OF PHYSICAL PUNISHMENT OR CORPORATE

The Bible, the word of God, allows the use of physical or corporal punishment (according to Proverbs 23:13-14). Nevertheless, parents should be careful not to use this method of discipline exclusively or excessively, as it can cause bitterness, anger and resentment on the part of children (according to Ephesians 6:4).

WHAT DOES DISCIPLINE INCLUDE ?

Discipline includes loving guidance of children and using corporal punishment only when other methods have failed. Don't ignore repeated occasions when your children disobey, because if you wait until you run out of patience, you will discipline them just to relieve your anger and not to correct their mistakes. On the contrary, discipline them when they have disobeyed, so that their disobedience does not become an established and accepted fact.

Do you think a parent shows love for their child when they discipline and correct him/her? When disciplining your children, it is also important that you, as parents, be considered as one authority in the eyes of your children. Do not make the mistake of defending your children when your spouse corrects them, because if you do, you separate authority within the household and your children will no longer know who to obey. On the other hand, the one who discovers a child's disobedience should be the one who disciplines him. Do not threaten the child by saying, "When your father (or mother) comes home, you will be spanked. If his disobedience requires him to be disciplined, do so immediately.

WHEN IS DISCIPLINE NECESSARY ?

When discipline is necessary, it is important to tell the child the exact reason why he or she has been disciplined and how he or she should behave in the future. After the punishment, the parent should show love, forgiveness and acceptance of the child. The child should never feel rejected even if his or her conduct is punished. Doesn't the Lord have an attitude of love, forgiveness and acceptance when we fall? (from Nehemiah 9:17; Micah 7:18; Luke 7:36-50)

COMMUNICATE WITH YOUR CHILDREN

In this circumstance, be sure to communicate with your children. Listen to their needs, ideas and even -- why not -- their complaints. An open ear will often help you prevent problems before they require discipline. Listen to your children and really consider their points of view, sometimes even in prayer. You will find that sometimes they observe things in life as well, if not better, than you do yourself!

LOVE YOUR CHILDREN

The apostle Paul teaches Christians to love their children (according to Titus 2:4). While it is true that good discipline is a form of love for children, it is not the only one.

Children should not grow up and be raised in an atmosphere where severity is the norm. The same hands you use to spank your children can often be used to caress them and show them your affection.

Sometimes children disobey simply to attract attention. Parents should be aware of this and show more interest in their children by providing them with a special moment dedicated to them alone. If parents are so concerned about their own activities that they have no time for their children, they may one day find that they no longer have any influence on them. From then on, the path to delinquency is not far off.

The servants of God should be exemplary, but they sometimes make the mistake mentioned above. Some love the Lord with an enthusiastic love and, as a result, work zealously for the salvation of sinners. But at the same time, they lose their own children. They are more interested in the salvation of others than in the salvation of their own homes!

What a sad truth that was found in the mouth of a believer about a young man who was living a life of sin: "He is as evil as the son of a preacher. "If you are a servant of God, do not let such a thing happen in your family. If you have a home, you may want to examine yourself and see how well you are doing as a parent.

Next to each statement below, mark an X in the free space under the proposal that best suits what you are doing in your home.

I do my parenting homework well
I teach the word of God to my children
I could do it better.
I teach obedience to my children

I need to put it into practice
I teach my children to work I teach stewardship to my children I discipline and correct my children
I show my children that we are, father and mother, one and the same authority.
I am an example to my children of what they should be. I treat my children with love and spend time with them.

THE HOME HAS A STEWARDSHIP ROLE

Prove examples of men who fulfill their responsibilities as stewards of their families. God is especially interested in the salvation of families (from Acts 11:14; Acts 16:31-33).

Once family members are saved, the steward should be the leader so that all can continue to serve the Lord. As you have already noted, the steward of the Christian home fulfils a dual role: he is both the husband of his wife and the father of his children.

The responsibility of the steward and especially the servant of God is to lead his family well (according to 1 Timothy 3:4-12). Let us now consider three aspects of this responsibility.

The steward is responsible to God for the integrity of his home. When an outbreak has been destroyed, in most cases it is the result of poor management.

The steward is also responsible for the conduct of his children. Like Anne, he should therefore consecrate them to her and ensure that they become her children (according to 1 Samuel 1:27-28). God desires the steward's children to become believers and to behave as such (according to 1 Timothy 3:4; Titus 1:6). Thus, God reprimanded Elijah for not having corrected his sons even though he had knowledge of their misconduct (according to 1 Samuel 2:22-36; and 1 Samuel 3:11-14). David's case was even more dramatic. He knew how to rule a kingdom with justice, but he didn't know how to rule his family.

THE STEWARDSHIP IS RESPONSIBLE FOR

The steward is responsible for the needs of his family God, as a good and just father, takes care of the well-being of his children. Within his household, the steward must make every effort to do the same. He has every reason to do so (according to Matthew 24:45), for if he does not care about his own, he acts like someone who has denied his faith and is worse than an infidel (according to 1 Timothy 5:8)

CHAPTER 4
THE CHRISTIAN FAMILY

Objective -

In following the suggestions given in this book, list some specific ways to use your home for the glory of God.

A PLACE FOR THE PRESENCE OF THE LORD

In some houses, there is a sign that reads: "Christ is the head of this house, the invisible host of every meal, the silent listener of every conversation". These words are good because they remind us of Christ's presence in our homes. With reference to them, let us check that everything is clean and in order, that the children are behaving well and that the conversation is healthy and uplifting. How great must Zacchaeus' joy must have been, as well as his haste to welcome Jesus into his house, the one who wanted to visit him (according to Luke 19:5-6). The feelings we have in our home should be even stronger because Christ is always with us.

Our home should be an oasis of joy and peace. Unfortunately, some believers seem to forget this. Rather, they believe that Jesus lives only in the Church, the place where their conduct is most holy. But their children are troubled by not being able to understand why their parents are not as holy at home as they are in the Church. A good way to make Christ's presence real in the home is to have a family worship service. At a certain time of the day, parents and children gather to study the divine word and worship God together. Thus, family worship will help both spouses to remain united and children to obey their parents in the Lord.

CHAPTER 5
THINGS TO BE DONE DURING FAMILY WORSHIP IN A HOME

A HAVEN FOR GUESTS

The Bible teaches us that offering hospitality to strangers in our homes is a real blessing for us. Indeed, some have done so in the past and have welcomed angels without knowing it (according to Hebrews chapter 13:2). After his conversion, Matthew offered a banquet and invited all his friends with Jesus and his disciples. He undoubtedly wanted his friends to know Jesus too.

We can do the same thing. We can invite a friend to our house to talk about Christ, a new Christian to encourage him in the faith, young people to share our experiences with them and brothers and sisters in general to strengthen our love and Christian communion.

A widow, who was a Christian, felt very lonely and depressed after losing her only daughter. One Sunday, she invited a young woman who was far from her native country and nostalgic for it to dinner in her house. They rejoiced so much that they got into the habit of spending every Sunday together. A very strong friendship developed between them and some time later, the young woman accepted Jesus as her savior. As stewards of God, we have the duty and privilege to offer hospitality to pastors, evangelists and other servants of God (after 1 Peter 4:9; Romans 12:13). Above all, the one who serves God should be characterized by a sense of hospitality (according to 1 Timothy 3:2; Titus 1:8).

THE HISTORY OF THE SUNAMITE

The Sunamite who prepared a room for the prophet Elisha gives us a wonderful example of this truth (after 2 Kings 4:8-11). In the New Testament, Lydia is another remarkable example of a woman's hospitality (from Acts 16:14-15). She showed her consideration by offering her house to the apostle Paul and to all those who travelled with him.

A CHRISTIAN MUST BE A WITNESS FOR THE LOCALITY

Let's talk about the Christian home. Christian households should be an example within their locality, in their neighborhood. They should be a testimony of what Christ can accomplish within a home. They should embody Christian virtues in their locality. At the time of the apostles, Christian households played an important role in the expansion of the Church. Groups of Christians gathered in houses to eat together (according to Acts 2; 46), to pray (according to Acts 12:12) or to hold evangelical meetings (according to Romans 16:5,23 and Corinthians 16:19; Colossians 4:15).

In fact, it can be said that the Church began to progress from Christian homes. In the same way, today's Christian homes can be like a lamp in the darkness, sending the light of the Gospel into their neighborhood (according to Philippians 2:15-16).

As in past centuries, many of today's churches began in the home of a believer. You can indeed offer your home to host evangelical meetings or a Bible study. Some of your neighbors who have never been to church may find it pleasant to hear the Gospel in your home.

A HAPPY MARRIAGE

How to build a happy marriage?

There is no such thing as a same-sex marriage. According to the Bible, the word of God, marriage exists between a man and a woman (according to Genesis 2:18-24). If there is a marriage between boy and boy, or between woman and woman, this marriage does not come from God, but from Lucifer, or from a government presided over by Lucifer. And this marriage is called abomination, corruption.

This is the marriage that God created. The man will have to cling to his wife, and they will have to become one flesh (according to Genesis 2:24). For the word of God, there is no divorce either (according to Genesis 2:18). This means that when the Creator, the Almighty God, instituted it, marriage was to be a permanent union between a man and a woman (according to Genesis 2:18). The Lord God still says: it is not good for man to remain alone, I will give him a help that corresponds to him.

Then God formed one with the side he had taken of man, and took it to him. Then the man said: "This is finally the bone of my bones and the flesh of my flesh. She will be called woman, because from the man she was taken. Therefore the man will leave his father and mother and must cling to his wife, and they will become one flesh.

Building a happy marriage is certainly not easy, but it is perfectly possible. Many couples have been happily married for 50, 60 or more years. How do they do it? They are continuously and generously involved in their relationship in order to "gain the approval" of their spouse. It takes a lot of effort. If you are willing to devote the necessary time and effort to it, you too can build a happy marriage that will last a long time. Carefully follow the instructions of a serious contractor.

A serious contractor would never start a project without consulting his plans. Likewise, we cannot build a happy marriage without carefully consulting God's instructions in this area. They can be found in the pages of the Bible, his word, which details the role of each of the spouses. "All Scripture is inspired by God and useful to put things in order," wrote the apostle Paul. Husband and wife can learn a lot from the way Jesus acted with his disciples.

Indeed, in the Bible, Jesus' relationship with those who will reign beside him in heaven is compared to that between a man and his wife. Jesus remained faithful to his companions, even in the most difficult times. He loved them to the end. As a compassionate leader, Jesus always took into account the limits and fragility of his disciples. He never demanded more from them than they could do or give. Even disappointed by his closest friends, Jesus remained gentle. He did not rebuke them harshly; on the contrary, following God's example, he tried to straighten them out with humility and kindness.

Therefore, if you consider the tenderness with which Jesus treated his disciples and how they responded to his love, you will learn practical lessons for building a happy union.

THE CHRISTIAN MARRIAGE MUST BE BUILT ON A SOLID FOUNDATION

Your marriage will inevitably go through difficult times, comparable to storms. These will test the foundations of your relationship with your spouse. The most solid foundation on which a happy marriage is built is a faithful commitment based on love. Jesus stressed the importance of this when he said: "Do not separate what God has united" (Word of life). Here, therefore, do not separate is addressed to both husband and wife, since they have made the vow to remain faithful to each other. Some may consider the commitment too binding. Today, personal convenience often outweighs the sacrifices of commitment.

MATRIMONIAL ENGAGEMENT

What can strengthen matrimonial commitment? The apostle Paul wrote: "Husbands must love their wives as their own bodies. To be united therefore means in particular to care as much for the well-being of one's spouse as for one's own. Married people should no longer think of "me" and "my", but of "us" and "our". By overcoming the attacks on your relationship, you will become wise. The wisdom thus acquired can lead to happiness. "Blessed is the man who has found wisdom," says the word of God.

A SOLID AND SAFE HOME

For a house to be solid and safe, it must be well built. Therefore, be determined to build your marriage so that it will last a long time. Use materials that will allow your fidelity to withstand the test of fire. Give great value to such priceless qualities as divine wisdom, generosity, discernment, fear of God, affection, gratitude and love for the laws of God, and true faith.

Happiness and contentment in marriage do not depend on material goods or professional success. They are built in the heart and mind. And they are strengthened by the truths contained in the word of God. May each one always be careful of the way he builds! This exhortation can also apply to marriage. What will the spouses do when the problems arise?

For a construction to stand the test of time, a good maintenance program is essential. When husband and wife regularly support each other in their goals and show honor and respect, their union remains strong. They do not let selfishness take hold and they control their anger. Conversely, lasting anger and frustration can kill love and affection within the couple. The apostle Paul advised men: "Husbands, continue to love your wives and do not be bitter against them". The same principle applies to women. When spouses strive to be considerate, kind and understanding, they contribute to the happiness and contentment of both.

Not rejecting the abrupt behavior, Paul urged his companions: "Become good to each other, full of tender compassion, forgiving each other willingly. And if a feeling of incapacity, a feeling of being underestimated, or exasperation are sources of tension, calmly, explain clearly to your partner what is on your mind. However, when it comes to minor issues, it may be better to let love cover them. A man who has been through hardship during his 35 years of marriage says that, even if you are very angry with your spouse, you should never "stop talking to him". And he adds these wise words: "Above all, never stop loving him."

You are able to build a happy marriage. It is true that building a happy marriage is not easy. But when spouses are determined to do everything possible to give God a place in their union, they experience happiness and security. So be careful about your family's spirituality, like a rock. And remember, as Jesus said, that the credit for a happy marriage goes to neither the husband nor the wife. It is first and foremost the responsibility of the author of the marriage, the Lord God. Those whom God has harnessed to the same yoke, let no man separate them!

TO HOLD A HAPPY MARRIAGE

It is necessary and sufficient to study the word of God as a couple regularly, and pray to God to help and guide you in solving your problems. You must also communicate freely, frankly and lovingly about your differences.

THE MEASURES TO BE TAKEN

Be kind and considerate when talking to your partner; ban angry outbursts, continuous remarks and hurtful criticism. Please humbly apply the Bible's advice, even if you feel that your partner is not doing everything he or she should. Do your best to cultivate the spiritual qualities mentioned in the Bible, the word of God.

CHAPTER 6
A HAPPY AND LASTING MARRIAGE

All marriages have it's problems, which can arise at any time. The important thing is to learn to deal with them gently and before they destroy the relationship. Here are the best tips and advice for a happy and lasting marriage. How to have a happy and lasting marriage?

First, marriage should be a marriage based on Christ. Regardless of your age, whether you are an old or newly married couple, there are some basic rules to follow. These rules will not always be easy to apply in practice, but they are important to do so. If you respect them, your marriage will be all the more solid and you will appreciate the good things in life together: pleasure, sex, trust, affection.

On average, twenty positive remarks are needed to compensate for the harm resulting from a single negative comment, a hard look or an impatient hum. Therefore, reinforce the positive and moderate the negative. Compliment your wife for her new shoes, your husband for his new blue shirt. Thank him for his participation in household chores. Call her at her office to tell her that you are thinking about her (especially avoid discussing household chores or children's bad grades).

Make sure that your compliments and thanks are sincere and specific: "I know that I can always count on you to keep my car safe and in perfect working order". "This tablecloth is very pretty. You always find a way to make our house a pleasant place. Look your partner in the eye when you smile at him or compliment him. Accompany a tender gesture with a happy smile. When you adopt this attitude, you realize that in addition to knowing how to irritate your partner, you know how to please him. After all, that's how the relationship began.

We also discover that there is still time to express our affection. When you come home at night, hug her and kiss her so she knows you're happy to see her again. On a rainy Sunday morning, surprise her by bringing her coffee in bed (and stay to chat with her). Know how to appreciate its qualities and ignore its defects. To let her know how happy you are to be with her, serve her your best smile when you bring the gift home. Make the resolution to kiss each other at length every night before going to bed. You do a lot of little things for your children; why not for your spouse?

TOUCHES

Touch helps to release endorphins. Pure happiness, in the one who gives as in the one who receives. Walk arm in arm on the way to the grocery store. When you kiss her in the morning, stroke her cheek with your fingertips. Relive these little gestures from your first moments together: a little kiss behind the ear, a hand through the hair, etc. Touch is a complex language and you will benefit from enriching your vocabulary.

UNDERSTAND NO ONE IS PERFECT

It is sometimes tempting to blame your partner for feelings of anger, disappointment, boredom or stress about your marriage. From there to thinking that, to improve your relationship, it is he who must change, there is only one step. This is a mistake.

When you try to change your partner, you put him on the defensive and you find yourself in the role of the hateful character. The result of the races: neither of them changes or takes responsibility for their actions, and the best because they no longer know how to appreciate and are less critical. And the two members of the couple regain the motivation to change in order to create even more joy. If an argument arises, try to change the subject, inject a dose of mood, show sympathy or show your partner that you appreciate him or her. If it's a waste of time, take a moment to calm down.

YOU HAVE TO CHOOSE THE RIGHT TIME AND THE RIGHT PLACE

In this regard, you should avoid difficult topics when you are tired or hungry, situations that can lead to unpleasant remarks or black thoughts. For the same reason, do not take intoxicating drinks during an argument for people who are not converted. It is not possible to discuss your marital problems if you are busy with something else. Good advice: if, for example, you have a discussion that has been raised among you, you should, in turn, turn off the television or computer, hang up the phone and leave everything you are doing. If you are distracted or need to go out, choose another time to talk. You can't solve a conflict while doing something else. It should not be underestimated that, at any given time, cries of helplessness could lead to insecurity and behavioral problems.

HAVE ATTENTIVE EARS

The best thing you can do to strengthen your relationship is to talk less and listen more. Reproaches, insults, criticism and intimidation can only lead to break-up or, at most, to an infernal life. When the conversation becomes a battle, give your partner the opportunity to express his or her feelings. There will always be time to propose a solution or defend yourself.

CHAPTER 7
LOVE, FALLING IN LOVE IS THE EASIEST THING

There are several ways to feed the woman. Love should not be ignored. This is from the Chief Creative Officer. Summer is here, weddings are in full swing and their music can be heard everywhere. Tears flow as we attend the ceremonies and watch these couples embark on a new life together. We often wonder if some of us would not cry over their lost dreams of great promises of love by remembering their own results. Marriages are unraveling, marriages that we thought would last forever. And those who maintain themselves are not really what they used to be. Marriage requires a lot of work. Falling in love is the easy part; the delicate part is keeping love vibrant. There are much better ways to look at it.

First, be positive. Who wants to live with a sad and negative partner? It's frustrating to have to share your life with someone who only sees the negative side of things. Sullen and closed faces or mood swings destroy the joyful atmosphere that makes the house a haven of peace. It is possible to create joy by developing the habit of looking at the world positively and having a good disposition. Start by smiling at those you love, even if you don't want to.

I know this may seem trivial, but you can't imagine the impact your face can have on others. Our wise men teach that when it comes to food, the whiteness of our teeth, when we smile at each other, is even more important than the whiteness of milk. Love flourishes in a positive atmosphere. So try to stop complaining and look on the bright side. You will see that your beloved will reflect your new attitude and will soon smile back at you.

Secondly, never speak in anger. If you feel anger boiling in you, it means that this is not the time to talk about what is bothering you. When we talk in anger, our emotions take over. We say things we don't mean, and say words we shouldn't. We raise our voices and lose control.

We have met too many couples who, in anger, uttered words that they later bitterly regretted. "This is too much, this is it, we're leaving! "We really should never have experienced it; what a mistake! "Maybe we should just get a divorce! ».

Even if, later, we try to justify ourselves ("that's not really what we meant, we were in a very bad mood"), the damage is done and the deep wounds don't go away.

Third, let us learn to give.

To love in Hebrew is called ahava, from hav, which means to give. The more we give, the more we love. Too often, we wrongly believe that the more we receive, the more we can come to love. We believe that it is the beautiful diamond ring, the priceless watch or the latest technological gadget received from our beloved that gives us the feeling of being special and loved. Of course, it is always nice to receive gifts. But that's not what makes love last. This only reinforces our desire to want more. We become lessees rather than donors. We are waiting for the next gift; we look forward to the next thing that will make us happy. And when we feel that we are not receiving enough, we become unhappy. Our love based on giving me more is starting to weaken.

A GREAT PIECE OF ADVICE TO YOU !

Make sure you grow your love by investing in your relationship. Do not let a day go by without giving of yourself, to better arouse love. Giving should not mean ruining yourself. Reach out with a word of encouragement, prepare a favorite dish, or send a message of love like that, for nothing.

Some people relax at home, neglecting their appearance, not making an effort for their spouse, but are always impeccable for others, for the outside world. What a mistake! Just take 6 minutes, brush your hair, change this t-shirt all stained and pull yourself together, remember, introduce yourself as you did on your first date. Show him that it is always important to you.

THE UNITY OF THE PERSON

It is easy to let ourselves be trapped and see only what irritates and annoys us. There is always a question: "Why can't he ever rid the room of what's lying around? Why can't she ever be on time? »

We easily forgive ourselves for our own mistakes. We swept away our shortcomings and decided that, overall, after all, we were not so bad. Why not do the same with our spouse? Think of three qualities you can find in your partner. (If you can't, then you have work.) The next time you find yourself focusing only on his bad habits that are so painful, engage immediately. Fill your mind with those qualities that make it so special. Do not limit your vision to what irritates you or you will end up missing out on all the blessings.

STOP COMPARING

It's about making arrangements to go on vacation together. Questions have always been raised: Why did her husband buy her discounts for their wedding anniversary? Why does his wife make him good little dinners when I have to have the same kind of meal every night?....

There is no worse poison than making comparisons. Others seem better off, more in love, happier, enjoying good times together... The truth is that you never know what goes on behind closed doors. He may have bought her jewellery, but she would like to see him spend more time with her and the children, as your husband does. And no matter how much she prepares all kinds of tasty meals for him, he still wants simple, relaxed dinners and interesting conversations, as your wife knows how to do.

Comparing is never healthy. Comparing gnaws/corrodes our happiness and takes away from us any appreciation of what we have. We become so busy looking at the lives of others that we neglect to see everything for which we should be grateful. By focusing on those around us, we are led to believe that we are missing something. We feel resentment without really knowing why and we always feel vaguely unhappy.

If I am able to create a life full of happy and dear moments, then I can survive even the most difficult days, because my best friend stands by my side. Together, we can build. Together, we can win. Do not let your blessings fly away, hold them firmly and bring the magic of peace into your home.

CHAPTER 8
HOW TO STAY IN LOVE ALL YOUR LIFE ?

INTIMACY

The word intimacy can be defined as the feeling that connects two people in what they may feel for each other. If you give yourself enough attention and everyone feels good, you feel close to each other. On the other hand, if one makes the other uncomfortable, a certain distance is created.

THE PSYCHOLOGY OF INTIMACY

Many books have been written on the psychology of intimacy and love. Moses' books provide us with a profoundly simple formula for creating and maintaining intimacy, based on the following notion: emotional intimacy depends on how we manage our negative emotions or those that disturb us. This formula is found in the book of Leviticus, chapter 19: 16- 19. It contains seven briefly listed commandments. These verses contain the fundamental psychological principles to stay in love for the rest of your life. While you are studying this formula, give yourself and your spouse a score on a scale of 1 to 10.

1 = lamentable failure; 10 = solid in excellence.

CLEARLY ESTABLISHED BOUNDARIES ARE NECESSARY TO PROTECT INTIMATE RELATIONSHIPS

This commandment warns us against the temptation to report what others say to someone else, especially if this information could hurt or harm them. The underlying principle here is to establish boundaries in order to protect your relationship from harmful external influences. Be careful what you say to others about your spouse. As a general rule, we advise spouses never to share their relationship problems with anyone unless they have received permission from their spouse. This is one way of setting good boundaries.

Another mistake, commonly made by couples, is to confide their problems to family members. Parents and in-laws should be kept away from your marriage. Parents must respect your privacy, and if they do not, it is necessary to remind them. Once married, your spouse becomes your number one priority.

CAREFULLY MONITOR EACH WORD SPOKEN

We are never allowed to hurt someone with our words. This is a simple idea, but it has profound implications. We are always responsible for what we say to others, especially to our spouse! Yet we can see many couples being carefree, making no effort in the way they speak, not attaching importance to the words spoken.

It is never good to call your spouse by degrading names, curse him or her, or even raise your voice if it will frighten or intimidate him or her. Imagine how many couples could experience greater love by following this simple rule. Each word exchanged with the other has a positive or negative impact on your emotions. If you want to stay in love, you must constantly monitor and control the way you talk to each other. There is no concept of time-out in a marriage; every interaction counts. Each word spoken will either bring you closer or further away from each other.

DO NOT BE INDIFFERENT TO THE DANGER OF YOUR PARTNER

Keep this principle in mind more carefully: do not ignore the emotional pain of the other. How do you react when your partner suffers or is in a bad mood? Are you annoyed, with little room for tolerance, or do you listen patiently? Most of us have a hard time withstanding bad mood, what I'm really saying is: I'm in pain and I need you, that you understand me and support me.

This commandment tells us that we have an obligation to be sensitive to the pain of others but certainly also to avoid causing them even greater pain if they are already suffering. It is never acceptable to ignore or attack someone who is suffering, especially if it is your spouse! How many times has he told you, "All right, stop it, stop it. » ? It's not just being insensitive, it's just cruel! One of the most profound needs of the human being is to be understood. When we ignore our partner's pain, we are far from giving him the impression of being understood. Every time we reject his pain without taking the time to understand it, we miss an opportunity to get closer to him. For one of the greatest acts of kindness that one can do to others is to listen to them without judging them. "Do not hate your brother in your heart. »

THIS IS THE PRINCIPLE

Do not reject or ignore bad feelings. You have a responsibility to solve problems caused by your negative feelings towards others. Biblical commentators emphasize that the importance of this commandment lies in the words in your heart. These words suggest that it is normal to have bad feelings, even feelings of hatred. Only Mr. Spock of Star Trek never has bad feelings towards others. Unfortunately, many people who grew up in emotionally unstable homes do not allow themselves not the expression of emotions, whether negative or positive. Some people believe that evolved people never have bad feelings.

This is not Judaism's view of human emotion. The Torah assumes that we will all have bad feelings towards each other, and that the solution is not to keep them in us, to make them simmer in our hearts. The problem is not having bad feelings, but not being able to manage them effectively! And the sine qua non condition for managing them as well as possible is the need to be honest with ourselves emotionally.

Sometimes we all feel bad feelings towards our partner. But if these bad feelings are not recognized and resolved, they become harmful and destructive. They must be identified and understood. Gnawing at each other's blood, feeling guilty or blaming others are ways to avoid taking responsibility for your feelings. There are four ways to explore and resolve your negative feelings: analyze them yourself, tell a friend, discuss them with your partner and, if the bad feelings persist, talk to a professional. One of the challenges of staying in love is to learn from these negative feelings towards your partner and to solve them, there are several principles.

WHAT CAN WE DO TO TAKE BACK OUR NEIGHBOUR?

Principle number 1 - When someone hurts you, let them know how you feel. We are not allowed to exclude people from our lives because they hurt us. Judaism requires us to establish a dialogue with those who hurt us and to strive to repair the relationship by speaking openly and honestly. In marriage, good communication means sharing with your partner what you are experiencing in order to repair the cracks in the relationship.

Principle number 2 - To be able to communicate, you must feel safe. When you talk about your feelings with your partner, he or she should be receptive, attentive and critical. Creating a safe environment to share your feelings is a prerequisite for open and honest communication. Do you feel safe with your partner? And do you give him a sense of security?

"You will not assume sin because of him." Exercising this principle means not allowing yourself to blame, accuse or insult your spouse. The famous biblical commentator, Rashi, interprets this commandment as a prohibition to expose someone to shame when we tell him how we feel. Being ashamed is one of the most painful feelings a person can have. That is why Judaism explains that embarrassing someone is as serious as spilling their blood.

There are three methods of communication. Some people never tell their partners how they really feel. This is the passive method, which only causes a lot of suffering and distance. It is obvious that one of the reasons that sometimes prevents a spouse from sharing his or her feelings is fear of the other's reaction. That is why it is essential for couples to learn how to create a space where everyone feels safe.

If you don't feel safe with your partner, you will never be able to tell him how you really feel.

The other method of communication, which is equally unacceptable, is aggression. Aggressive people only know how to scream and get angry to express their feelings. This is obviously not very effective and in many cases it becomes abusive.

The right method is assertion. Assertive communication means that you can tell your partner how you feel without provocation. Assertive communication also gives you the opportunity to be heard and understood. The best you can do is to express your feelings honestly and talk with respect to your partner. He then has the choice of listening to you or ignoring you, but you will at least have done what you were supposed to do, which is to express yourself with confidence and confidence. One of the most important tools for a good relationship that couples should have to succeed is what Dr. John Gottman calls the "ability to repair damage".

Assertive communication is the essential tool to repair any damage. This is considered repaired when no resentment, anger, or bad feelings persist. This means that if the conflict is resolved one hundred percent, ninety percent is not enough. If you have 50 conflicts and you only repair them at 90% each, you still have 10% grudge, multiplied by 50. These small amounts can accumulate very quickly, and where bad feelings persist, the relationship weakens and love disappears. The problem is rarely the real problem. Communication to deal with the problem is the real problem! A lasting love is built on an assertive communication.

"DO NOT AVENGE YOURSELF OR HOLD A GRUDGE."

Principle number 3

If you don't eliminate the "old quarrels" once and for all, you will continue to do so, and you and your spouse will hurt each other. Unfortunately, too many couples do not repair their damage 100%, which results in dozens of harmful feelings and unresolved problems that will never be closed cases. When old wounds are not fully healed, they tend to become infected and love begins to fade. This commandment informs us of the two ways people try to make the person who makes them suffer : suffer revenge and resentment. Revenge in marriage means doing the same thing or giving back to your spouse. This can mean that they are no longer helped, no longer pleased, for example, deprived of intimate relationships, affection, or any act of kindness. How often do couples use the weapon of silence, live in entrenched camps or attack each other, accusing and complaining? The many aspects of revenge will, of course, extinguish the flames of love.

Another way to make the other person suffer, in our turn, is resentment. We hold a grudge when we say to our partner, "Well, I'll help you this time, but don't think you're going to get away with it so cheaply with what you've done to me again. Or: "I will help you, because I don't want to lower myself to your level".

LOVE DOES NOT BOAST, LOVE YOUR NEIGHBOUR AS YOURSELF

Principle number 4.

When we resolve our bad feelings towards others, we create space for love. The fact that the commandment to love one's neighbor comes last in this list proves the truth of this principle: love and intimacy cannot flourish and grow in a negative atmosphere. Bad feelings must be identified and resolved if you want to stay in love for the rest of your life. It is always easier to ignore our feelings or try to justify them so that we don't have to think about them anymore. But this approach never works! The difficult path, in fact the only one, is to identify and understand these problematic emotions and take responsibility for working on them. You must commit to being emotionally honest with your partner and yourself. If you do not feel the love you would like to feel, it is because you and/or your spouse continue to have negative feelings that have not been effectively treated.

The late Rabbi Noah Weinber defines love as the pleasure experienced when we identify the other with his qualities, while accepting him with his defects. Feelings such as anger, resentment, shame, isolation and guilt cloud our ability to see the good side of the other person.

Negativity always obscures positivity. You must create a place for love by removing all that is negative, to be able to constantly recognize and appreciate in your partner the qualities that bring about this love.

CHAPTER 9
THE BAD CONCEPTIONS
OR
ATTITUDES OF PRAYER

The bad attitudes or conceptions prevent us from effectively interacting with our Creator through the scriptures. There are several points to note:

The first point or flap; I feel like I'm talking to a wall. Since we do not see God, nor do we perceive him through any of our five senses, we are reluctant to engage in a conversation with him. A one-way dialogue is strange at best; at worst, it borders on madness.

2nd part

A quoi bon prier Dieu s'il connaît mes besoins ? De deux choses one, it is argued: if we need something, God will give it to us; if not, he will refrain from doing so. How can prayer change his mind?

3rd part

God does not seem to answer our prayers. Sometimes we pray for a patient, but the patient still dies. Similarly, we pray for years to find a spouse or to have children, and our requests are not granted. So what is the point of continuing our efforts?

4th part

FORMAL PRAYER IS A CHORE

How can you have a natural conversation with others if you can't decide what to talk about, or when to start the discussion? This is not called communication. Let's look at each of these blockages and see how a slight change in perception can make all the difference.

A BAD IMPRESSION

I feel like I'm talking to a wall. Most people believe in the power of prayer. Late for an important appointment, looking for a parking space, before an important exam, if a close relative or friend is ill, we instinctively whisper a prayer and ask for help. This is proof that we believe in the presence of a supreme being. How many times have you talked to someone on the phone, without giving them the opportunity to say a word for a good half hour in a row?

You spoke without losing the thread of your thoughts, in a passionate and inflamed tone, without seeing or hearing the person on the other end of the phone! Knowing that your interlocutor is listening to you, you have succeeded in creating a magnificent monologue! So? No, it is not the absence of a tangible interlocutor that is at the root of our loss of interest in prayer. Rather, it is our difficulty in admitting that God is real and what a tremendous opportunity we have to be able to talk to Him.

Imagine that the President of the United States gives you a telephone interview tomorrow morning at 9 a.m. sharp, and that he is ready to devote twenty-two minutes of his time to listening to your concerns and answering all your questions. Is there any chance that you won't wake up in time the next day or that you decide to do something else at that time? God, who is far more powerful and benevolent than the most influential of men, has given you his personal telephone number and is waiting for your call. When you pray, think for a moment about the fact that you are currently in conversation with the master of the universe.

ANOTHER HIGH POINT

What's the point of praying to God if he knows my needs?

On the sixth day of creation, before man was created, it is said: "and every plant of the field before it was in the earth, and every herb of the field before it grew : for the Lord God had not caused it to rain upon the earth, and there was not a man to till the ground." (Genesis 2:5)

This verse is surprising, because on the third day of creation, we read: "And the earth brought forth grass, and herb yielding seed after his kind, and the tree yielding fruit, whose seed was in itself, after his kind: and God saw that it was good" (Genesis 1:12). Where had the plants created on the third day gone, when the sixth day arrived?

Rashi, a famous commentator of the 11th century, solved this difficulty: "Since there was no one to appreciate the benefits of rain, God kept the grass and trees under the surface of the earth until the appearance of man, who prayed for the rain. Then it rained and the plants grew (according to Genesis 2:5). This is a profound aspect to consider. God had always intended to allow man to enjoy fruits and vegetables, plants and trees. But he waited for the man to ask for it and only then did he grant it. God has created needs for us because he wants to forge a relationship with us. He wants us to turn to him.

Moreover, seeing all your needs met is not necessarily a blessing. In the account of Adam and Eve, God curses the serpent for his participation in the original sin: "You are the most cursed of all creatures. You will crawl on your belly and feed on the dust of the earth" (according to Genesis 3:14), one would think that the snake would get away with it. After all, his food is abundant everywhere and he just has to crawl on the ground to feed himself! But the commentators explain to us the true content of this curse. In essence, God said to the snake: I never want to see you or hear from you again. Take whatever you need. And now, disappear forever from my sight. Make the Lord your delight, and he will give you what your heart desires. Certainly, God knows our needs. But he wants to forge a deep relationship with us. After all, he is the one who can fill all our gaps. In other words, he wants us to turn to him, recognize his presence and realize that he is the source of all our needs.

WOULDN'T GOD SEEM TO ANSWER OUR PRAYERS?

It is imperative that we change our perspective in this regard: God is listening, but it is up to us to decipher his answer. Sometimes the answer is: no. Sometimes it is: not right away. Or: work on your patience, or another trait of character and turn to me again. We must determine whether our request is really beneficial for us in the long term. If so, we may be asked to improve in one area in order to get what we want. God is not a candy vending machine.

Any request from us is the beginning of a dialogue. We must learn to identify God's answers, try to understand and accept them, and then reassess our own choices. Continue to make your requests, while trying to integrate the messages he sends you, and to strengthen your faith and attachment to him.

THE INTEREST OF A FORMAL PRAYER

What is the point of a formal prayer?

Imagine that you have to prepare a key presentation to a committee of directors in order to obtain a major grant. It is obvious that you will take notes to ensure that you do not forget any important details. In addition, you will probably be delighted to receive excellent advice from experts in the field, who are familiar with the tricks of the trade. Just as when you address the CEO of a large company, when you speak to God, it is imperative that you clarify your requests and the reasons for them, in order to obtain maximum results.

The sages of the great assembly, composed of giants from the books of Deuteronomy and Leviticus, wrote the main prayers found in the Jewish prayer book, giving us the model ritual to adopt when we address God. This pre-established text highlights three essential aspects of prayer: the awareness of the supreme being to whom we turn; the nature of the requests that should be addressed to him; and the duty to recognize God's blessings towards us. If they were recited according to our moods or our own assessment of our needs, it is very likely that our prayers would be incoherent and inconsistent. Our sages offer us insider secrets: here are the essential things you should ask him, here is what really matters! Formal prayer is the starting point for our dialogue with God. But this dialogue should not end there. We must infuse our personal feelings and demands into the ritual, and appropriate its terms. Without this, prayer is limited to the mechanical recitation of a script, like the monotone speech of a telephone solicitor. Where is the sincerity? Where is the attachment? It is up to us to look up from our notes to speak freely to God, to express our deep desires, our own wishes and feelings, through the formal ritual. This process requires preparation, as with any important speech.

Allow yourself a few minutes at the beginning of the day, and think about your personal needs. Then take a look at the Amida prayer, the main prayer that includes 19 blessings covering all the dreams and needs of the Jewish people: health, livelihood, wisdom, redemption, peace, etc. Take your list of needs, find the corresponding blessings, and integrate your own words into the blessing, in your own language and with your own thoughts and nuances.

For example, your son behaved badly and you now expect a difficult conversation with his teacher. In reciting the blessing of reason, you could intersperse the following personal prayer: "Please help me to find the words that will prevent this child from being expelled from his class at all costs; please, let the teacher perceive the causes of my child's difficulties, and grant us both the necessary discernment for the best possible solution for the parties involved".

CHAPTER 10
AN ANSWERED PRAYER

YONA LEARNED THE ART OF JEWISH PRAYER: A GREAT STORY

Someone was studying by phone with Yona, a living woman in Tel-Aviv who claims to be non-religious. The week before, she had told him that she was going through a difficult financial period and would have liked so much to increase her income in order to have a morning off to study in Jerusalem on a regular basis. The man in question got up one morning, very early and discussed the problem with God. What does he say to her? What is certain is that on the same day, at 14:00, two new customers made an appointment with him! Since then, they have committed to consult it regularly and have already recommended it to others. He didn't even know how to pray, but his prayers were answered! He was very impressed by this testimony. Here is a woman who claims to be non-religious, but who, in spite of everything, does not hesitate to get up at dawn to pray. And the most beautiful thing is that she was not even surprised to see her prayer answered.

He has given much thought to this entity that you call God and here is the conclusion he draws from this belief in an infinite being: He can do whatever he wants, all the power of the world is in his hands and he hears it when he talks to her. How can we deprive him of such a dream opportunity to speak to him?

Now Yona has understood the art of Jewish prayer. Immediately, she turned to God, fully aware of his presence and power; she clarified her requests and the reasons for them; and she addressed God directly and sincerely, in her own words, and then waited for the answer.

On this basis, we can all be inspired by Yona. Let's pick up the phone. God is waiting for our calls. How to get an answer to your prayers? Do you intend to speak to an image when you pray? We will indicate to you the possible ways for your prayers to be answered.

First of all, let us make one thing clear: God is always ready to answer our prayers. He is our father in heaven, and we are his children. He loves us unconditionally, even when we offend him. Then why does it seem to us that God does not take our prayers so much into account? And since he already knows what we want, why is prayer necessary in the first place?

INFINITE LOVE

Even those who stay away from the synagogue intend the existence of God. As the saying goes, there are no atheists in a trench. When a guy is lying inside and the enemy arrives, he always shouts: "God Almighty, get me out of here, we want to live! ». What does he actually say? "Dear God, although we have ignored you all these years, denied your existence, and not appreciated at all, everything you have done for us, we are in a lot of trouble now and we know that you are the only one who can help us. »

To pray properly, you must understand that not only does God love you, but that His love for you is infinite. God has given you eyes, ears, intelligence, life itself! Every morning, Jews recite the blessings of grace to God for the gifts given. These blessings are there to remind us how much God loves us. Indeed, if we really appreciate what God has done for us, we didn't care about not staying in constant contact with him. Someone wondered why we need to pray. When we pray, it is obvious that we do not explain anything new to God. He doesn't need us to remind him what we need. So why not simply explain our requests to God through our deep need to pray? Prayer itself helps us to refine and affirm what we want from life. It is a real process of maturity. If a billionaire father gave his son unlimited cash on a silver platter, he could only become a spoiled and irresponsible child as he grew up. If God had given us everything automatically, we would never have been able to define for ourselves what we want in life. Certainly, life would be easy for us. But we couldn't grow up.

Since God has our interests at heart, he wants us to achieve our goals with the sweat of our brow, because that is precisely what will make us grow. Why do we have problems in this world? God has all the right connections. It can solve your financial problems. So why do we have all these problems? Because no matter how brilliant or powerful you are, you will never be able to live your children's lives for them. Because to bring an authentic love to your children is also to allow them to develop personally and become independent.

If we were only robots, working mechanically and according to instructions, the world could be clean and tidy. But life would have no meaning or meaning. We have free will, the ability to make decisions that are eternally valid. We can choose to distance ourselves from God and he himself will let us do it.

No, because he wants this to happen, but because he wants us to be independent, even at the risk of misusing that independence.

THE ANSWER TO YOUR PRAYERS

Have you ever had an answered prayer? Stop for a moment and consider all the implications. You live in America, in a small town in the Midwest. There is an extremely large and unsightly pothole in front of your house. For the past four months, the local municipality has ignored your insistent requests to have the problem resolved. So, in an outburst of frustration, you call the White House and ask to speak to the president. (It's worth a try!) To your amazement, the president himself picks up the phone. You explain yourself quickly about your problem. The president listens for a minute, then hangs up.

You don't really expect anything to be done about it. The next morning, you look out your window and, surprisingly, the Army Corps of Engineers is busy repairing your road.

So the president took your request seriously and sent his troops to help you! This means that, in order for your prayer to be answered, you must be able to reach the president directly. And, who is the only person who can always reach the president? The president's son, of course. This is the nature of our relationship with God: a father and child relationship. As a parent answers his child's requests, so God answers prayers. The Infinite Giant who created each molecule on this earth, can modify up to the course of existence in order to answer your prayer.

To truly speak to God, you must know that he is willing and able to do everything. Otherwise, you will only be dealing with a finite concept of God and not with our true father in heaven. We want to insert here the story of an atheist's prayer, a true and authentic story.

On his return from a trip to Japan where he had visited his Japanese fiancée, Wilson stopped in Jerusalem. He decided to visit the Wailing Wall to admire the old stones. Upon his arrival, he felt, surprised, something heavy and very moving. Wilson then stood in front of the wall and composed an atheist's prayer. He looked at the stones and said, "God, I do not believe in you, and as far as I know, you do not exist. But I feel something. I want you to know, God, that I have absolutely nothing to say against you. I just don't know if you exist. But, God, just in case you're really here and I make a mistake, give me an indication.

As Wilson ended his prayer, a student from Jerusalem saw him and thought he might be interested in learning a little more about this monument. "What the hell do you want from me," Wilson shouted. "Sorry," replied the student, "I just wanted to know if you want to learn more about God. So, Wilson had just finished his prayer by asking for an indication, and immediately someone offered to present it to God. Certainly, the Almighty is close to all those who call upon him in truth (according to Psalms 145:18).

There are several reasons why you must be sincere with God. Be sure that God can help you. Everything you ask him will always be infinitely small compared to what he has already given you. If you do not expect good, God will not invade your space. He wants you to connect with your heavenly father and yet he also wants you to work to earn it.

By not answering you, God tells you that you have a problem, that you need to change. For that, he is doing you a great favor. Because if he didn't, you would get stuck in your illusions and not be clear with the idea that God can do everything. Yes, he can do anything. Heaven and earth belong to him. The Almighty can organize for you a plan, whatever it is, as long as you believe in him. He knows how to get our attention. When we forget that he loves us, he sends a red light to refocus us.

God has no need and does not need a relationship with us. We're the ones who need a relationship with him. Our greatest pleasure is to be in contact with God. That's why he organizes small misfortunes to get our attention. All this for our own benefit.

We have seen, for example, Luke's interest in the hearts and minds of men. He even reports debates in the form of a soliloquy: that of the unjust steward: "What will I become since my master is taking away my stewardship? I don't have the strength to work the land; I would be ashamed to beg. I don't know what I'm going to do (according to Luke 16:3-4). Or the prodigal son's: "My father's employees have plenty of food to eat and I'm here to starve! I am going to my father's house (according to Luke 15:17-18)".

Then everyone acts: the steward shows indulgence towards his master's debtors, the prodigal son returns home. The inner determination is translated into conduct. Luke therefore deals with two parts of the tripartite structure (God, the heart of man, and his conduct) where goodness exists. If we suspect him of being light on the first of them, we are right. It is light on God, but not negative. God is above all else. The best thing human beings can do is not to speculate on divinity (it is more the Johannine accent, which is heavily theological), but to deal with the crises they face; for such crises are the key points of the historical process, which, for Luke, is theology.

To do what is necessary in the face of historical necessity is to obey God. The rich man in the parable, in Luke chapter 12: 16-21, is a fool because he does not take into account that the wheel turns and takes revenge. He assumes that the accumulation of assets is stable. For Luke, it is a form of atheism: "This is the case of one who makes reserves for his own profit, but who is not rich according to God (according to Luke 12:21)".

He uses the commonplace of Old Testament wisdom, according to which atheism is the height of madness, and the phases of history and its crises constitute God's relationship with humanity and humanity with God. For Luke, repentance is, at the same time, adjustment to unfavorable circumstances and knowledge of God. In its narrative form, it is perhaps the Summum bonum, the first necessity of historical beings.

LUKE'S WRITINGS

We can confirm what we have already observed about the form of Luke's ethics and also have other insights by comparing it with Mark's writings.

Matthew testifies to a concern for human interiority similar to that of Luke, in each of the antitheses of the Sermon on the Mount: "You have heard what was said to the elders... Well, I'm telling you. "(According to Matthew 5:21-48). The new ethic is an inner disposition: not to be angry or lewd, not to swear or ruminate on one's resentment, to love. From what we see, in Matthew, there are good and bad people. Sometimes the wicked disguise themselves as good, the wolves as lambs, but these efforts are in vain, because the actions that are born of their inner dispositions, their moral fruit, betray them (according to Matthew 7:15-20).

Luke, on the contrary, shows ambiguous people, both good and bad, whose actions are not so much moral works that will be held back by the ultimate censor at the last judgment, but rescue operations that translate into survival and vivacity in the present and, after all, in some future.

NUANCES BETWEEN LUKE AND MATTHEW

The differences between Luke and Matthew are a matter of nuance and development. Between Luke and Mark, they are more extreme. Mark's determinism contrasts with the importance of human choice in Luke: not exactly freedom of choice -- Luke is too realistic to assume anything like that -- but the ability to change within the constraints defined by circumstances. In the book of Mark, the divinity takes over, leads the action to its designated end and no one can do anything about it. The result is a dark simplification, as in the parable of the sower (according to Mark chapter 4: 3-20), in which men are reduced to types of terrain; and in his somewhat forced convention of the invincible foolishness of the disciples. But there is also a tragic force of paradoxical depth. According to the chapter in the book of John 14:21, the son of man must leave. It is written. But woe to him who helped deliver it. It would have been better for him if he had never been born.

THE GOOD AND THE EVIL

Good and evil in John's gospel, considered the last canonical, are understood within his cosmic vision: the light of the divine being shines in the dark world of becoming (see the prologue according to John chapter 1). Good is inherent in eternal life, participation in Jesus and the father. Evil refers to staying out of it or, worse still, in the outer darkness. Waiting, staying is good, apostasy is bad. When, in the trial and death of Jesus (according to John chapter 18 and 19), good and evil meet, Jesus is impressively stable at the moment when his traitor, his accusers, his judges and even his disciples swirl around him in a worried agitation.

CHAPTER 11
WHY ARE THERE SO MANY BLOCKAGES IN THE CHRISTIAN HOME ?

The apostle Paul wrote a famous chapter on the agape. This word is translated as love, charity, in 1 Corinthians, chapter 13, where he alluded to the three opening clauses of the form: I can and I can Y, but without love, I am nothing. According to 1 Corinthians 7:4-5, four clauses follow, beginning with love.

The first with two positive verbs: love is patience, love is benevolence; the second with a negative verb: love is not jealous; the third with five negatives: it does not boast, does not swell up, does not hurt, does not seek its interest, does not take evil into account (according to 1 Corinthians 7).

Verse 5 and a proposal converse (his joy is the truth); followed by four positive verbs whose object is everything. The last clause (love never falls) is opposed to the weaknesses of prophecies. It is then the partial that is opposed to the perfect, the child to the man, the enigmatic at Moses' face-to-face meeting (according to Number 12: 8); finally come the three immutable ones: trust (pistis), hope (elpis) and love (agape), of which the last, love, is the greatest.

In other words, why are there so many blockages in the Christian home? According to 1 Corinthians, chapter 6, verse 14 says: And God, who has risen also by his power. And verse 15 has a great climax and says, do you not know that your bodies are members of Christ, to make them members of a prostitute? Far from it! Don't you know that the one who attaches himself to the prostitute is one body with her? For, it is said, the two will become one flesh. Verse 17 tells us that he who clings to the Lord is with him one spirit.

In this question, there is no longer the word divorce. If you do, it concerns you, but preferably do not get married, or try to reconcile with your spouse to have another peace. For Christ said in his word: No one can break what God has united.

Don't listen to leaders who say you can get married again: that's not true. Divorce is not for the Christian (according to Genesis, chapter 2: 18 and Genesis @: 24; Ephesians 5: 32-33.

For the blockage, read 1 Corinthians chapter 7. Verse 3 states: "Let the husband give back to his wife what he owes her, and let the wife do the same to her husband. The head of the universe has spoken, you must listen to him, otherwise you cannot go to heaven, period, that's all.

BENEFICIAL ADVICE FOR CHRISTIAN HOUSEHOLDS

According to Ecclesiastes, chapter 4: 12; Ephesians, 5: 29-31; 1 Corinthians 7: 2-5, if one thinks he is strong, he will find two others who can beat him. And a rope that has three wires can easily break.

Thus, in his perfect plan, God placed the Christian home as a holy life on earth. From the creation of the world, it was God's plan that the home should live in happiness, joy and love. His will was not that the homes should break up, but rather that they should live and remain solid.

While the Lord of Lords foresaw a perfect peace for the home, Satan the devil who is the most cunning of all the animals in the field, was able to attack this plan in a criminal way. The Bible, the word of God, invites us to get rid of all the old attitudes that are problems in the home.

When two people join together to form a home, they are bound forever or until death separates them. When two young people are engaged, they make their efforts to become angels, flawless and spotless. When, for example, two people marry, small trifles sometimes arise between the two spouses, in the husband or the wife.

As Christians, you must declare it openly in order to be able to convince Satan the devil. For victory is ours," said God, the Lord of hosts. Remember that you are adults and not small children. You must settle your business with each other.

MONEY IN A HOME

The issue of money is a big problem that is eating away at Christian homes.

Sometimes the husband manages to accumulate and hide his money; the wife also does the same. Do not forget what the word of God tells us in John 2:24. We are no longer two, but one. There must be no indifference between husband and wife. Money can't divide you for that. There may be times of trouble and discouragement. But as a Christian who awaits the coming of Christ, you only have to overcome them in prayer.

In the book of Matthew, chapter 12: 43-45, it is said: when the unclean spirit has come out of a man, he goes through arid places, seeking food, and he finds none. Then he said: I will return to the house from which I came out; when he arrives, he finds it empty, swept and decorated. He goes away, and takes with him seven other spirits more evil than himself; they enter the house, settle there, and this man's last condition is worse than the first. It will be the same for this evil generation.

This idea is one of the reasons why homes can be uncontrolled or wasted, because there is misunderstanding in sexual life.

BAD FRIENDS/COMPANIES

In the home, there are sometimes bad companies. The Bible tells us that bad companies corrupt morals. You have to be careful because bad friends drag you in the wrong directions or on the wrong slopes. Bad friends never have good words until they want to guide you to perfection. But you can find good people who will guide you in the right direction (from Psalm 133).

The Christian's home must resemble the kingdom of Christ. In the book of Job, chapter 34, we find the following words: For the ear perceives the words, as the palate tastes the food. Let's choose what's right, let's see what's right between us. Job continues: I am innocent, and God refuses me justice; I am right, and I appear to be a liar, my wound is painful, and I am sinless. Listen to me, you sensible men! Far from God injustice, far from the Almighty, iniquity!

He gives back to man according to his works, he rewards everyone according to his ways. Certainly, God does not commit iniquity; the Almighty does not violate justice. Who charged him with governing the earth? Who entrusted the universe to his care? If he only thought of himself, if he took away his mind and his breath?

DIVISION COMES FROM THE DEVIL

Corinthians chapter 1: 10-11: I exhort you, Brothers, by the name of our Lord Jesus Christ, to speak the same language, and not to have divisions among you, but to be perfectly united in the same spirit and in the same feeling. For, my brothers, I have heard about you from the people of Chloe that there are disputes among you.

THE DEVIL IS THE AUTHOR OF DIVISION, BUT JESUS-CHRIST IS THE AUTHOR OF UNITY

There is a great truth in the word unity. We do not see the pronoun Me, but rather Us. For, it is said that the self is hateful and proud (according to 1 Corinthians 11:3). The pronoun is ours considered as the Christian home. The Christian is the example of Jesus Christ. The pronoun we, here, typifies the brothers and sisters as a whole, the Church of Jesus Christ. That is why the Bible, the word of God, prescribes fraternal love for us. There must be peace, decorum, patience, tolerance, etc. between us. No, no scandals.

For the word union, it covers the idea of homeland. In this perspective, there are sometimes people of different characters who are not referred to in the same direction.

There are people who only breathe violence. Some even have a thought of betrayal, to the point of wanting to organize a coup d'état. That is what we have to consider in the word union. Somewhere in the Bible, especially in Genesis 1:26, it says: "Let us make man in our likeness or image, and let him rule over the fish of the sea, over the birds of the air, over the cattle, over all the earth, and over every reptile that creeps on the earth.

God created man in his image, he created man and woman. This means that in God there is no error and division. More like love and decorum. And it says: me and my father are one. Here, it is the unity that exists, not the division. Therefore he who wants to be glorified by God the Father in heaven, must walk as the child of light, because Christ is light.

SOLOMON'S WISDOM

After an introduction highlighting the determination, even the cruelty with which he consolidates his authority, the Solomon who appears in the next eight chapters looks like a different man.

No violence or intrigue of any kind tarnishes the image of the wise and victorious king, whose main concerns are the extent of his commercial domain and his ambitious construction projects, including that of a temple worthy of his God. Throughout this section, a short narrative drama unfolds.

The story of two prostitutes, in 1 Kings Chapter 3:16-28, is the only episode marked by a certain tension, and the only text where Solomon intervenes directly. Elsewhere, he simply receives praise and honors from God and man, and holds in his hands an opulent empire whose prosperity is not threatened by anything.

In Chapters 3 and 4, the emphasis is on Solomon's wisdom. In a vision, in Gabaon, God promised him the knowledge necessary to judge the people and "discern good from evil". The story of the prostitutes illustrates his wisdom in action: not only is the king able to find the truth, but he does justice that is a source of life: Give the woman the living newborn, and especially do not put him to death (after 1 Kings 3:27). Unlike what happened during David's reign, the kingdom is at peace, "everyone under his vine and fig tree" (1 Kings 4:25, according to the editions), and Solomon receives a tribute from the neighboring peoples. His glory is considerable.

CHAPTER 12
THE ETERNAL IS TIRED OF THE WORLD AND WOULD LIKE TURN HIS BACK

THE CASE OF SODOMUS AND GOMORRAH

The sin of man appears to be disobedience and a serious violation against God the Creator. In Chapter 3, this sin raises the daunting question: "Will the image of God be preserved in us? "She receives a positive response in the composition. Man, now called Adam, transmits the image of God to his offspring on this point. In this same strategy of man's sin, God has never ceased to seek him out in order to forgive him, despite his weakness and inconsistency.

In Genesis, chapter 13, verse 13, we see that the people of Sodom were very evil and sinful towards the Lord. He blinded them all the way to the entrance of the house, from the (smallest) to the (largest), so that they took unnecessary trouble to find the door. In the same vein, this verse provides us with a legal directive that prescribes an exact balance between capital crime and punishment.

THE LORD IS TIRED OF THE WORLD

Many contemporary governments agree with gays and lesbians and enact laws in their favor.

According to the Bible, the word of God, it is a kind of abomination, and an insult to the Lord of hosts. Who will live, will see. These types of governments will be punished by the eternal lake of fire. In 1 Corinthians, chapter 6, verses 8 and 9, it is said: But you are the ones who do injustice and rob others, and they are your brothers! Do you not know that the unjust will not inherit the kingdom of God? Make no mistake about it; neither adulterers, depraved people, homosexuals, thieves, greedy people, drunkards, insults, and hoarders will inherit the kingdom of God.

ABOMINABLE THINGS

The false balance is in horror to the Lord, but the right weight is in his favor. When it comes to pretentiousness, there also comes contempt; but wisdom is with the humble. The integrity of the upright leads them, but the perversity of the traitors turns to their desolation. Fortune is useless on the day of wrath, but justice delivers from death. The righteousness of the upright man makes his way straight, but the wicked falls by his wickedness. The justice of the upright delivers them, but by their greed, the traitors are trapped. When the wicked man dies, his hope perishes, and the power he expected is lost. The righteous is delivered from distress, and the wicked comes in his place (proverbs 11:1-8).

The wicked covets the net of evil men, but the root of the righteous bears fruit.

In the midst of laughter the heart can suffer (proverbs 14:13) and, in the end, joy can become grief. For the Lord hates the perverse man, but his intimacy is for the upright men; the curse of the Lord is in the house of the wicked, but he blesses the dwelling of the righteous.

But he who pursues evil ends in his death, a man who loves wisdom rejoices his father, but he who frequents prostitutes loses his possessions. Justice elevates a nation, but sin is the shame of peoples (proverbs 14:34). In this 21st century, it is not surprising to see even so-called evangelical leaders, priests or pastors associating themselves with the practice of homosexuality and encouraging or training people to use it. This practice is common worldwide. For them, it's a joke of the flesh. Did God create humanity in this condition? Since the fall of Adam and Eve, the earth has experienced such a bad slope. Although humanity has been forgiven by the birth and resurrection of Jesus Christ, man continues to live outside the will of the creator, namely the great Almighty God.

IN BENIN, THE PEOPLE CELEBRATE VOODOO
THE ORIGINS OF VOODOO

Voodoo, recognized since the pregenesis, is one of the oldest religions, dated more than fifty-four million years ago. Voodulants often question evil spirits. Voodoo (voodoo, or voodoo), more rarely called voodooism, is a religion originating from the former kingdom of Dahomey in West Africa.

THE VOODOO

Comments from a reader. We know from experience how long it takes to get a clearer picture. All sources of evidence acknowledge the Celtic part of the cultural and political heritage of the trading posts. This project is enshrined in Haitian law and is considered a benefit of colonization. It is like a fair that lasts even through voodoo worship as a ritual.

HAÏTIAN VOODOO

The Haitian practices voodoo magic. And he knows how to make a voodoo doll. Despite its name, a voodoo doll does not really originate from this cult, but from ancient techniques of witchcraft with a doll.

Man in general, instead of seeking the presence of God in prayer, seeks to do the technique of witchcraft with a doll. See how to use a voodoo doll. When he is making the doll, he thinks about the person he is trying to enchant and how to convince. This doll is made in a paranormal way, that is, it is represented to apply the laws of interaction. Even Haitian heads of state are using it. In this sense, I, Pastor Raymond Saintil, remember writing a letter on Tuesday, April 15, 2003, to the President of the Republic of Haiti. Here is the content:

Mr. Jean Bertrand Aristide,
President of the Republic of Haiti
National Palace
Excellency

We, the group of Haitian pastors from Orlando, Florida, United States of America, are very pleased to send you this letter to congratulate you on the way you have taken on the responsibility of managing this country, our native land. The national promotion of the nine departments will restore hope to the Haitian mass, bourgeoisie and diaspora.

Our duty is to help and encourage the work of government for the benefit of future generations. Therefore, as leaders concerned with the Holy Gospel of the Lord and Savior Jesus Christ, we want to prevent you from falling into disgrace.

We are referring here to your recent decree officially establishing voodoo in the public interest. In our opinion, this is an unfortunate decision that has never happened in the entire history of Haiti, from the founding of the country to this present generation. It is also an insult in the eyes of God and in the eyes of the nation. And if this decree is promulgated, Haitians run the risk of being called voodoo dogs by the international community. And there is no doubt that the Lord, for his part, will strike severely against the government in power and its immediate collaborators.

Excellency, our primary objective is to see a Haiti for Christ and Christ for Haiti. And as you already know, we love you very much. That is why we have launched prayers to God, manifested throughout American cities, in the company of Christians and non-Christians, and joined our efforts to make your physical return to Haiti a reality.

If then, by the grace of the Most High, you have been able to return to the National Palace, you should in return glorify the Lord. And as in St. John Bosco, you should prescribe the Holy Bible as a reference, and not encourage Haitians to put themselves under the yoke of Satan.

Mr. President, before concluding, we would like to remind you that when some kings of the Old Testament ruled their country at will, the Lord struck them with leprosy. We will also mention the case of Nebuchadnezzar, who was transformed into an ox, and even wanted to eat grass for a period of years.

Far from wishing you such a fate, we will only specify that the sword of the Lord hangs on the heads of all those who transgress his laws. We therefore encourage you to work in perfect union under the guidance of the Holy Spirit of God for the prosperity of the brave Haitian people. And we leave you to meditate on verse 14:2 Chronicle, chapter 7.

Mr. Speaker, I assure you of our unwavering commitment.
Signed: Pastors and Churches.
The president of the Evangelical Leaders United of Central Florida: Pastor Raymond Saintil.

THE LAST JUDGEMENT BEFORE THE GREAT THRONE OF THE COURT OF CHRIST, WHAT WILL HAPPEN?

The day of judgment: what is it about? What does the Bible teach? The judgments of God. What are the different judgments that will take place before the final judgment?

What does all this have to do with each other? The Book of Revelation shows that the day of judgment will begin after the Har-Maguedon war, when Satan's system on earth will be destroyed.

THE DAY OF JUDGEMENT

The day of the last judgment (or day of the Resurrection or day of the Lord or day of Retribution) is, according to Abrahamic religions.

REVELATION - OPEN BIBLE

For more details, read the book about the prophet Daniel, chapter 8 and following, and listen to the programs on the apocalypse.

The last judgment, apocalypse 20: 11-15

"Then I saw a great white throne and the one sitting on it. Earth and heaven fled from him and no one was found. place for them". Christ encourages and promises reward to faithful Christians. "To the victor, I will make the victor eat of the tree of life placed in God's paradise". (Revelation 20:7-15) - The Last Judgment (Revelation 20:2)

THE IDEA OF HELL IS VERY DISTURBING

What is the White Throne Judgment? The judgment of the great white throne is described in Revelation 20:11-15. This is the final judgment, at the end of which the lost will be thrown into the Pond of Fire.

Revelation 20:7-15 tells us that this judgment will take place after the millennium and that Satan, the beast and the false prophet will have been cast into the lake of fire. The books that will be opened (Revelation 20:12) will contain the works, good or bad, of everyone. For God knows all that we have ever said, done, or even thought of, and he will reward or punish everyone accordingly (Psalms 28:4; Psalms 62:12; Romans 28:4; Revelation 22:12).

At the same time, another book will be opened: the book of life (Revelation 20:12), which will determine whether a person will inherit eternal life with God or suffer eternal punishment in the lake of fire.

Although Christians are held responsible for their actions, they are forgiven in Christ and their names have been recorded in the book of life since the creation of the world, according to Revelation 17:8).

We also know from the scriptures that on the occasion of this judgment, the dead will be judged according to their works, and that "all those who were not found recorded in the book of life" will be thrown into the lake of fire and brimstone.

Many biblical passages confirm that there will be a last judgment of all men, believers or not. Each person will stand one day before Christ and will be judged for his works. While it is perfectly clear that the judgment of the great white throne is this last judgment, not all Christians agree on its connection with the other judgments mentioned in the Bible, especially those that will be judged on this occasion.

Many Christians believe that the Scriptures reveal three distinct judgments to come. The first is the judgment of the sheep and goats, or the judgment of the nations (according to Matthew 25:31-36). Which would take place during the tribulation, but before the Millennium, to determine who will be able to enter the millennial reign.

The second is the works of believers, known as the tribunal or Bema, of Christ (after 2 Corinthians 5:10), in which believers will receive rewards for their works or service to God.

The third judgment would be the judgment of the great white throne at the end of the Millennium (from Revelation 20:11-15), when unbelievers will be judged according to their deeds and condemned to eternal punishment in the lake of fire.

Other Christians believe that these three judgments refer to a single final judgment, not three separate judgments. In other words, believers and unbelievers alike will be judged on the occasion of the judgment of the great white throne, described in Revelation 20:11-15. Those whose names are in the Book of Life will be judged according to their works, in order to determine the reward they will receive or lose; the others will be judged by their works to determine the punishment they will receive in the lake of fire. Proponents of this theory believe that Matthew 25:31-46 is simply an additional description of the judgment of the great white throne. They emphasize that the result of this judgment is the same as that of the great white throne. The sheep, the believers will enter eternal life, while the goats, the unbelievers, will go to eternal punishment (according to Matthew 25:46). Whatever our point of view on this subject, it is important to never lose sight of the facts regarding the upcoming judgment(s).

First, Jesus Christ, the judge, will judge the unbelievers, who will receive punishment according to their deeds. The Bible clearly states that unbelievers gather anger against themselves (according to Romans 2:5) and that God will treat everyone according to their actions (according to Romans 2:6). Believers will also be judged by Christ, but since the righteousness of Christ has been imputed to them and their names are written in the book of life, they will be rewarded, not punished, for their works.

According to Romans 14:10-12, we will all stand before God's throne of judgment, and each of us will be accountable to him for our actions.

CHAPTER 13
NATURE RISES UP AGAINST US

(1) NATURAL DISASTERS
(2) EARTHQUAKES ALL OVER THE WORLD
(3) TORRENTIAL RAINS
(A) STORMS
(B) CYCLONES
(4) FIRE

NATURAL DISASTERS

Why are there so many natural disasters in the world? Disasters of all kinds are constantly making the news. They are killing more and more people. The research centre on the epidemiology of things. Are disasters a punishment? The Bible, the word of God, does not teach that God provokes the natural disasters that are in the news. And the divine punishments she talks about have nothing to do with that kind of thing. Disasters precede a reconstruction phase (such as storms, earthquakes and tsunamis) and sometimes cause natural damage.

Similarly, insect invasions, fires and epidemics are among them. They differ from technological disasters, caused by both sides.

TYPES OF NATURAL DISASTERS FROM MANY EXAMPLES

Natural disasters have always been part of human history. A natural disaster is an increasing phenomenon, an event of natural origin, sudden and brutal, which causes major upheavals. It can have dramatic consequences (human or animal victims, material damage). These phenomena are numerous and difficult to classify. However, geological, climatic, biological, ecological and other disasters are usually distinguished.

GEOLOGICAL DISASTERS

They include earthquakes, landslides (as well as avalanches), tsunamis and asteroid collisions. An earthquake is a tremor of the ground (or a series of tremors) of varying intensity. There are about a million of them a year, but not all of them are murderers. They are caused by the deep release of enormous accumulated stresses, which results in the sudden and discontinuous movement of two blocks along a fault.

Landslides are a series of natural phenomena: falling rocks in a mountain corridor, mudslides mixed with boulders, slow deformation of a slope over several years, subsidence of the ground during an underground void filling, etc. The term landslide is used. Landslides are common and represent, in France, the second natural risk, after floods.

A volcanic eruption is the rise and spread of magma on the surface. This phenomenon, always very spectacular, however, does not have the same dangerousness according to the type of eruption (lava flow, fiery clouds, etc.). It is estimated that 270,000 people have been killed by volcanic eruptions since the 17th century.

The earthquake that struck Haiti on January 10, 2010, is a tsunami (from the Japanese tsunami: port wave). It is a wave generated by a deformation of the ocean floor due to an underwater earthquake (volcanic eruption or landslide). Waves, spaced a few minutes to an hour apart, can cause flash floods, torrential rains, hurricanes, tornadoes, etc.

Natural disasters, linked to man-made disasters, cause considerable loss of life and material damage, and cost more than $306 billion as of 20 December 2017.

Anyway, the Lord God uses these natural disasters to teach humanity a lesson. The latter, for its part, must learn these lessons in order to respect the greatness of the Creator. Nature itself has neither hand nor foot, but it is talked about by the power of humanity's great creator. When, for example, an event of this magnitude occurs in a small nation, large nations believe they are safe. However, everyone is under the control of the great creator, no one is spared on this point.

So try to humiliate yourself. Everyone is a sinner in the eyes of the Lord. There is no one who does good in the Lord Jesus Christ. Is there a secret abduction? However, the word rapture is not found in the Bible, but let us note that the saints meet Christ in the nakedness of the atmosphere. The rapture of the Church (or rapture) is an event of Christian eschatology would be transported to heaven. As always, this delight is inevitable in the existence of the planet. It is the expression of mystical ecstasy (The Christian art of counter-reform has emphasized the mystical rapture of the Saints.) The state of someone who is transported with joy, admiration, enthusiasm. (1 Thessalonians chapter 4, verses 16 and 17). The Lord himself, at a given signal, at the voice of an archangel, and at the sound of the trumpet, will come down from heaven, etc.

First epistle to the Thessalonians:
   A) The Practical State of the Thessalonians: Chapter 1
   B) The Apostle Paul's Ministry: Chapter 2
   (C) Timothy's Mission and Report: Chapter 3
   (D) The walk of believers in holiness: chapter 4, verses 1 to 12.
   (E) The coming of the Lord: chapter 4, verses 13 to 18.
   (F) The Lord's Day: chapter 5, verses 1 to 11.
   (G) Practical instructions to believers: Chapter 5: 12 to 28.

MOTIF AND MAIN THEME OF THE EPISTLE

The Thessalonians lived in permanent expectation of the return of the Lord Jesus (according to chapter 1, verse 10). They knew that he, rejected him, would publicly establish his kingdom on this earth with power and glory. In their eyes, this moment of the manifestation of his power was so alive that they were waiting for him every day. But during his visit, Paul apparently did not explain to them that before the establishment of this kingdom, believers had to be taken away first, and then returned to appear with the Lord. In any case, this point was still unclear to them. When some of them died, there was great concern that the deceased would have no part in the establishment of the Kingdom. Paul enlightens them on this subject, and that is the reason for his letter.

In chapter 4, he says: "But we do not want you, brothers, to be afflicted like others who have no hope" (verse 13). Then he clearly explained to them that the Lord would come first to awaken those who had fallen asleep and to take them away together with the believers who were still alive. There is therefore no prejudice for those who have already fallen asleep.

In chapter 5, the apostle again returns to this point, saying: "That we may either wake or sleep together with him. " (Verse 10). During our study, we will see that these are both living believers and those who are already with the Lord. This teaching concerns the coming of the Lord, who undoubtedly forms the central subject of the epistle, and is capable of encouraging and edifying us (chapter 5:11). This coming of the Lord is mentioned in all the chapters, each time under a particular aspect (chapter 1: 9-10). Here, the coming of the Lord is presented as the foundation of our practical life. This hope, the expectation of the Son of God from heaven, is an essential character of Christian life. Our lives must be oriented towards this goal. The Lord's return is not a theoretical knowledge; it influences our journey, our actions and our thoughts (chapter 2: 19,20). Paul relates the coming of our Lord Jesus to the reward or crown that the servant will receive. When Jesus appears, it will be revealed what each one of us has been for him on this earth (chapter 3: 12-13). The believer's walk should be characterized on the one hand by love and on the other by holiness.

When we think of the appearance of the Lord with his own, practical holiness, that is, the consecration to the Lord associated with the separation of all evil, should naturally follow (chapter 4: 13-18). Not only do these verses contain important teaching, they are also a precious consolation for those who have lost a loved one. We will be forever with the Lord, near him who loved us so much. Paul ends by saying: "Comfort one another with these words. In chapter 5: 1-11, the current of thought in the chapter continues here for the believer, the coming of the Lord is a subject of consolation and encouragement; for the unbeliever, it means an inevitable, terrible and eternal judgment. What solemn words! Amen. 1 Thessalonians 4:16 - "For the Lord himself, at a given signal, at the voice of an archangel, and at the sound of God's trumpet, will come down from heaven, and the dead in Christ will first rise again. »

Isaiah 25:8,9 - "He will destroy death forever; the Lord God wipes away tears from all faces, and makes the reproach of his people disappear from all the earth; for the Lord has spoken. »

Matthew 16:27 - "For the son of man must come in the glory of his father, with his angels; and then he will give back to everyone according to his works."

Matthew 24:30-31 - "Then the sign of the Son of Man will appear in heaven, all the tribes of the earth will mourn, and they will see the Son of Man coming in the clouds of heaven with power and great glory. »

Matthew 25:31 - "When the son of man comes with all the angels, he will sit on the throne in his glory. »

Matthew 26:64 - "Jesus answered him: you said it. Moreover, I tell you, you will now see the son of man sitting at the right hand of the power of God, and coming in the clouds of heaven. »

Acts 1:11 - "And said: Galilean men, why do you stop looking into heaven? This Jesus, who has been taken up into heaven from among you, will come in the same way as you saw him going to heaven."

2 Peter 3:10 - "The day of the Lord will come as a thief; in that day the heavens will pass away with a crash, the elements will dissolve in flames, and the earth with the works it contains will be consumed. »

Revelation 1:7 - "Behold, he comes with the clouds. And every eye will see him, even those who pierced him; and all the tribes of the earth will mourn for him. "Yes, amen!

Numbers 23:21 - "He sees no iniquity in Jacob, he sees no injustice in Israel; the Lord his God is with him, he is his king, the object of his joy. »

Zechariah 4:7 - "Who are you, great mountain, before Zerubbabel? You'll be flattened. He will lay the main stone in the midst of the cheers: Grace, grace for her! »

THE MYSTERIOUS MARK OF THE BEAST

What do they say about this mark? Who will receive it? How can you avoid it? It must not be a mystery!

The mark of the beast is prophesied and mentioned in the Bible. The question is this: is it a bio-chip implanted under people's skin? Or is it an ultra-thin electronic tattoo on people's foreheads? Is it your social security number or your passport number? Is it a geo-location device or a thought-controlling implant? Theories are well underway to determine the nature of this sinister brand.

Many people tremble when they read these verses: "And she made everyone, small and great, rich and poor, free and slave, receive a mark on their right hand or on their forehead, and no one can buy or sell, without having the mark, the name of the beast or the number of its name" (Revelation 13:16-17).

The Scriptures warn that this beast, whose followers are identified by a mysterious mark, will perform great miracles to seduce humanity, working hand in hand with a powerful military and political system. This system will be identified by the mysterious number of 666 (Revelation 13:18). All those who accept the mark of the beast will defy God! The apostle John wrote that each individual bearing this mark will also drink wine of God's wrath, poured unblended into the cup of his wrath (Revelation 14:9-10).

We must undoubtedly take this warning seriously!
What will this brand be? How will it affect you and your family? As the period of unrest that will mark the end of this era approaches, these questions are essential!

THE ANCIENT ROOTS OF A FAKE CHURCH

The Scriptures describe an ancient religious system, a mystery: Babylon the Great, the mother of prostitutes and the abominations of the earth (Revelation 17:5). This mystery has its origin in the ancient mystery religion of Babylon. Described as a prostitute, an apostate church, it is in direct opposition to God. The Scriptures describe a system that exerts great political influence and exchanges with world leaders (verses 1-2).

Further on, John describes this mysterious Babylon as a very rich and prosperous church, adorned with gold, precious stones and pearls. She held in her hand a golden cup, filled with abominations and the impurities of her prostitution (Revelation 17:4).

Jesus Christ seriously advised his people to move away and not to defile themselves with this church. Kadash, in Hebrew, which means: come out from among her or them, my people, so that you do not share in her sins, and that you have no part in her plagues (Revelation 18:4).

But why, nowadays, should a church be named after an ancient mystery: Babylon the Great? Because the teachings of this church come directly from the mysteries of ancient Babylon that are at the origin of most of the world's pagan practices (The worship of the Drad, J. Garnier collection, 1909, page 8). And one of the fundamental aspects of this ancient pagan religion was sun worship.

A RETROSPECTIVE OF THE WORSHIP OF THE SUN

In the days of ancient Israel, sun worship was widespread in the countries surrounding Palestine (Sun worship of anger's Bible Dictionary, page 1049).

God expressly warned the Hebrews against this form of idolatry, knowing that it would be a strong temptation for them: "Watch over your soul, lest, when you look up to heaven, and see the sun, the moon and the stars, all the army of heaven, you be trained to bow down before them and worship them" (Deuteronomy 4:19).

God is an invisible spiritual being (John 4:24). He created the sun to provide physical light and warmth to the earth and its inhabitants, not to be worshipped. God must be worshipped, but not his creation (Romans 1:25)!

The book of Revelation told us about the mark of the beast. It is very important to come back to this now. Currently, no one has the mark of the beast, but those who oppose it will be considered as cultists of the worst kind. Society is being manipulated to multiply and, in the not too distant future, receiving the mark of the beast will be the popular thing to do. Let me tell you, the mark of the beast and the seal of God are direct opposites.

There are two ways to know what the mark of the beast is. When Jesus Christ returns, the categories of individuals who will seek to hide correspond to those who have agreed to receive the mark of the beast.

Although no one has yet received the mark of the beast, it is already possible to see the danger on the horizon. God warns us not to take the mark of the beast, otherwise our punishment will be eternal damnation. It would just be enough for us to avoid taking the mark of the beast, to fight demons, plagues and the Antichrist himself. Despite the conflicts, the search for pleasures and the chaos that characterize this world, all will be encouraged to receive either the seal of God or the mark of the beast. Those who choose the latter will be thrown into the lake of fire.

666

The number 666, the mark of the beast, has caused a lot of ink to flow. Throughout the centuries, researchers of all categories have sought to identify the beast of recent times by means of its number. We know, in fact, that the Greeks and Romans (as well as the late Hebrews) used the letters of the alphabet as numerical signs. The addition of these signs gave a total. For example, we found the following inscription: "The one I love has the number 545". Thanks to this process, many people began to calculate, from existing names, the amount that could be arrived at.:9

If any man worship the beast and his image and receive his Mark in his forehead, or in his hand, The same shall drink of the wine of the wrath of God which is poured out without mixture into the cup of his indignation and shall be tormented with fire and brimstone in the very presence of the holy angels and in the presence of the Lamb: And the smoke of their torment ascends up for ever and ever: and they have no rest day nor night, who worship the .^ beast and his image, and whosoever« receiveth the mark of his name .

REV. 14 :9- 11

Thus, for 666, Nero, the Pope, Mohammed, Napoleon or Hitler could be identified as the possible biblical Antichrist. Our purpose, through this article, will not be to move in this direction. We would only be wrong, as those who preceded us in this process.

There is, through the biblical text of Revelation, something else to discover about the mark of the beast. This teaching is only accessible to those who take the trouble to compare it with other biblical texts in which the same symbolism appears: a mark on the hand or on the forehead.

SATAN'S THRONE AT THE VATICAN WEIRD THE MAJOR TEACHING OF THE APOCALYPTIC TEXT.

What John's text shows is that in the time of the Antichrist, the mark imposed on the hand and forehead of the Beast's subjects will be a condition of survival. No one will be able to buy, sell or do business without this brand on them. This mark is, at the same time, a universal identification system. It is not forbidden to think that it will be first and foremost that of the people of the Party of the Beast. Then, when it reaches absolute power, it will be imposed on all the inhabitants of the earth as a means of absolute control of the peoples.

The mark of the Beast is not to be assimilated with an identity card, even a magnetic one, which can be lost or falsified. It will be totally personal, affixed to the very body of those who wear it. It will be an indelible, inimitable mark that will allow immediate identification of its wearer. It will be almost impossible to refuse it because any activity related to life cannot be done without it. If it were only a kind of population control, the children of God, at the very least, in obedience to the authorities, could submit to it. But the brand will be more than that! It will be, said John, a sign of allegiance and adoration to the Beast. It is those who bow down to the Beast and his image who receive a mark on their foreheads or hands (Revelation 14:9).

Revelation 16:2: Nowadays, the physical mark of the Antichrist does not yet exist. There is no need to present our hand or forehead to identify us. But the marking has already started. This is a conditioning that will gradually lead to thinking and acting according to the orders of the Antichrist.

John tells us that the spirit of the Antichrist is already in the world. Through a slow process of conditioning, he will lead all humanity to worship a man in whom they will see their salvation. Once this has been completed, physical marking will be carried out without difficulty.

http://www.ncregister.com/daily-news/pope-francis-first-easter

https://stlucifer666.bandcamp.com/releases

REPETITION OF THE MAIN LINES OF REMARKS WE WILL HAVE TO MAKE FOR THE RETURN OF THE GREAT LORD JESUS ALMIGHTY

One of the greatest efforts to be made to meet the Almighty in a not too distant future is sanctification. One can then ask oneself this question: what is sanctification? What does that mean?

Although it is not often used in everyday conversation, it is a word of enormous spiritual importance! In other words, it is not only a subject of rhetoric for theological discussions. This is a very important subject in the eyes of God and for Christians. If we are not sanctified, we will not be able to receive eternal life. And neither will we be able to enter the Kingdom of God. Therefore, it is essential to understand the meaning of sanctification.

THE MEANING OF SANCTIFICATION

In the Old Testament, the Hebrew word translated as sanctifying is qadash, which means to consecrate, consecrated thing, to purify, purification, saint, holiness, celebrate, prepare, or choose (Strong's Hebrew Lexicon).

In the New Testament, the Greek word translated as sanctification is hagiasmos, which means separation, setting aside (Unger's Bible Dictionary).

To summarize the meaning of sanctification, this same dictionary continues: "The dominant meaning of sanctification is therefore separation of profanity and sin, and setting it apart for a sacred purpose.

Who sanctifies? Who carries out the separation, the setting aside, the consecration? God reveals himself as the one who does it. Let us note this that he said to ancient Israel: "You shall not profane my holy name, that I may be sanctified among the children of Israel. I am the Eternal One, that sanctifies you" (Leviticus 22:32). Just as God sanctified it physical nation of Israel, Jesus Christ sanctifies and consecrates his people today. "For he who sanctifies and those who are sanctified are all from one. That's why he's not ashamed to call them brothers.
(Hebrews 2:11)

Let us also note what the apostle Paul wrote to the Thessalonians: "For us, beloved brothers of the Lord, we must continually give thanks to God about you, because God has chosen you from the beginning for salvation, through the sanctification of the Spirit and by faith in the truth."
(2 Thessalonians 2:13)

God has chosen his people to inherit salvation through the sanctification (which distinguishes its people from what the Bible calls world) by his Spirit and by the truth. This highlights the relationship between the salvation and sanctification.

SANCTIFIÉD ISRAEL

Why did God sanctify the nation of Israel? He tells us this in Exodus 19:6, "You will be to me a kingdom of priests and a holy nation. He separated a people from the surrounding nations to make them his own people, a holy nation, a nation of priests, a model nation, his heritage, his children. Long before this alliance on Mount Sinai, Israel's choice as a holy nation had begun with Abraham. God had already said to Abraham: "Go away from your country, to the country I will show you. I will make you a great nation." (According to Genesis 12:1-2)

Later, when God changed Abram's name to Abraham's, he promised him: "I will establish my covenant between me and you, and your descendants after you, according to their generations: it will be a perpetual covenant, by virtue of which I will be your God and that of your seed after you. I will give you, and to your descendants after you, the land where you dwell as a stranger, the whole land of Canaan, in perpetual possession, and I will be their God." (Genesis 17:7-8)

God honored his promise to Abraham, and led his descendants to the promised land.

Just before entering it, Moses summoned the people and said to them: "You are presenting yourself to enter into the covenant of the Lord your God, in this covenant made under oath, which the Lord your God is dealing with you this day, to establish you today for his people and to be himself your God, as he told you, and as he swore to your fathers, Abraham, Isaac and Jacob" (Deuteronomy 29:12-13).

Finally, we must be sanctified by God: "To those who are called, who have been sanctified in God the Father, and kept by Jesus Christ" (Jude 1:1).

Sanctification is a process that begins when a person responds to God's call to believe in Him, repent and be baptized. God accomplishes three things when a repentant believer is baptized: "And that is what you were, some of you. But you have been washed, but you have been sanctified, but you have been justified in the name of the Lord Jesus Christ, and by the Spirit of our God" (according to 1 Corinthians 6:11).

First we must be purified by God of sin. Then we must be sanctified or set apart by Him to be saints. Third, we must be declared innocent in the eyes of God. All this is essential to begin our new life in Christ and to receive our final salvation in the Kingdom of God.

THE TRIUMPHANT CHURCH

The beginnings of the Church.

The beginnings of the Church are described in the book of Acts of the Apostles. This is why this course on the Triumphant Church focuses on the study of this book. This could be entitled "The Acts of the Apostles through the Power of the Holy Spirit" or "The Acts of the Holy Spirit through the Apostles". It is impossible to study the beginnings of the Church or the book of Acts of the Apostles without learning who the Holy Spirit is.

The book of Acts should never be studied as a simple historical book, but as a manual containing God's plan and purpose for the Church today. God has not changed his model or method. We must seek to reach those around us and the whole world as the first disciples did. Today we have received the same power given to the first believers.

The date of the writing of the book of Acts of the Apostles.

The book of Acts of the Apostles was written around 63-65 A.D., and it covers 30 years of ministry.

This study is not a complete and exhaustive study of the Book of Acts, but it focuses on the beginnings of the Church and the teaching we can draw from it for the Church today.

THE REVEALED TRINITY

The Old Testament teaches us about God the Father. In studying the New Testament, we observe the work of the Son and the Holy Spirit. In the Gospels, the second person of the Triune God is revealed to us. Jesus, the Son, reveals the third person: the Holy Spirit. The study of the book of Acts of the Apostles will lead us to an intimate knowledge of the Holy Spirit.

WARNING OF THE MARK OF THE BEAST

So the serious business is about to begin. They are already well underway. The New World Order is coming into being and much faster than we expected. It can be said that it has really started since the concept of "War on Terrorism" first appeared in 2001.

September 11 did not take place through the operation of the Holy Spirit. Machiavellian brains had drawn up the plan a few years earlier. The New World Order must be. The problem was that very few people would have seen it coming. By this we mean that out of 6.5 billion inhabitants, the real enlightened ones are only a few million. And again! The famous war on terrorism, created from scratch, is in fact aimed only at setting up a gigantic dictatorship. A global dictatorship. You have not been unaware of all the libertarian laws that have been implemented in the United States following the planned attacks of September 11, 2001.

These laws apply in particular to Muslims living in the United States, but also everywhere else. In London, Berlin, Paris, all over Europe, you only need to be a little tanned to be entitled to have your papers displayed. And then there were the biometric passports that were introduced with a lot of personal data included.

What does the brand of the Beast really represent?

In the book of Revelation, the Lord warns us against those who will take the mark of the Beast: "If anyone worships the beast and his image, and receives a mark on his forehead or on his hand, he too will drink wine of the wrath of God, poured without mixture into the cup of his wrath, and he will be tormented in fire and brimstone, before the holy angels and before the lamb" (Revelation 14:9-10).

Succubus Demon
https://hellhorror.com/demon-name-598/Succubus.html

This woman, called Succubus or Philomise, is very active in nocturnal sexuality.

Anti-christian - Are Catholics idolatrous?

The whole explanation about the worship of saints:

The idea that Catholics are idolaters is widespread in Christianity. Those who accuse the Catholic Church of the crime of idolatry, all quote the same verse, namely Exodus 20:4-5 where God says: "You shall not make yourself any carved image (...) You shall not bow down before these gods and serve them,." Reading this verse, it is clear that the Catholic is a pure idolater. It is therefore appropriate to give an explanation of this verse in order to kill error and misunderstanding.

Elsewhere, we have the indication that this brand will be imposed on a large number of people and will have significant economic and social implications, both for the rich and the poor, since it will be impossible to buy or sell without this footprint.

Revelation 13:16-18 - "And she made all, small and great, rich and poor, free and slave, to receive a mark on their right hand or forehead, and that no one could buy or sell, without having the mark, the name of the beast or the number of its name. This is wisdom here. Let him who has understanding calculate the number of the Beast. For it is a number of men, and its number is six hundred and sixty-six.

As Christians, it is obvious that we must do everything possible to avoid receiving this mark. But to do so, it is necessary to understand what it really represents. Several hypotheses have already been put forward as to the meaning of this brand.

Some have seen the mark of the beast in the barcode system, because the three lines at the ends and middle of the code are three 6. Others have seen it in another very popular technology today: the computer network.

The Internet itself is made in such a way that we are obliged to use the www code to access the websites. However, the transcription of this code into numbers represents, in the Hebrew language, the number 666 (triple v).

Subsequently, other more efficient technologies have also raised concerns among Christians who are concerned about avoiding this mark. First, there is the electronic chip imposed by our governments on official documents, such as identity cards, mutual insurance cards and bank cards. This chip is supposed to store administrative data such as civil status, residence address, socio-professional status, etc. in memory.

At the time it was promised that no private and confidential data would be included on the chip. A false promise! Recently, we have been talking more and more about a more secure and forgery-proof electronic chip (micro-chip), since it is placed under the epidermis of the arm or hand. This chip, the size of a grain of rice, will store all of the individual's administrative, medical and banking information.

A simple pass in front of the scanner will identify us, credit or debit our bank account. Of course, this system is not yet imposed. But it is operational and is already used in certain circumstances such as, for example, by some discotheque customers who prefer to pay for their tickets and drinks via this system. This avoids seeing them and losing money. So, is there anything in this list that would be the mark of the beast?

The word mark comes from the Greek charagma which means: sign or mark printed, sculpted, engraved, chiselled or incised. In the Bible, this word is usually translated by sign, except when we talk about the beast: the translators then choose to use the word mark. So the term, as we understand it today, would mean a physical mark on something. But if we analyze other biblical passages, we will see that this term can also have a figurative meaning.

Indeed, when we study the Bible, we see that it does not only speak to us of the mark of the beast, but also of its opposite: the mark or sign of God. To fully understand the mark of the beast, we must therefore analyze its opposite: the sign of God. In Exodus, it is written that the Passover will be like a sign on the hand and like a memory on the forehead: Exodus 13:9: "It shall be for you as a sign on your hand and as a memory between your eyes, that the law of the Lord may be in your mouth; for by his mighty hand the Lord brought you out of Egypt".

In Deuteronomy, it is advisable to attach the commands to the arm and forehead so as not to forget them. Of course, this is said in a figurative sense: the forehead being, as everyone knows, the centre of memory, and the hand or arm the member of the action.

Deuteronomy 6:8 - "You shall bind them as a sign on your hands, and they shall be like fronts between your eyes".
Deuteronomy 11:18 - "Put these words in your heart and soul that I say to you, and you shall bind them as a sign on your hands, and they shall be like fronts between your eyes".

In addition, the Sabbath, which is the 4th commandment, is also considered as a sign or mark that makes it possible to recognize the true servants of the Almighty:

Exodus 31:13 - "Speak to the children of Israel, and tell them: you will not fail to observe my words, for it will be a sign between me and you and among your descendants, that they will know that I am the Lord who sanctifies you.

Finally, in the book of Revelation, a clear distinction can be made between those who have received the mark of the beast and those who keep the word of God and the testimony of Jesus. We find these words in it: "And the smoke of their torment rises for ever and ever; and they have no rest day or night, those who worship the beast and its image, and whoever receives the mark of its name. This is the perseverance of the saints, who keep the commandments of God and the faith of Jesus.

Revelation 22:3-4 - "There will be no more anathema. The throne of God and the Lamb shall be in the city; his servants shall serve him and see his face, and his name shall be on their foreheads. So just as people will bear the mark of the beast, believers will bear the name of God on their foreheads.

Revelation 15:2 - "And he said: I saw as a sea of glass, mixed with fire, and those who had overcome the beast, and his image, and the number of his name, standing on the sea of glass, having harps of God".

And Revelation 20:4-6 - "And he said: I saw thrones; and to those who sat on them was given the power to judge. And I saw the souls of those who had been beheaded because of the testimony of Jesus and because of the word of God, and of those who had not worshipped the beast or his image, and who had not perceived the mark on their foreheads and on their hands. They came back to life, and reigned with Christ for a thousand years. The rest of the dead did not come back to life until the thousand years were fulfilled.

This is the first resurrection. Blessed and holy are those who share in the first resurrection! The second death has no power over them; but they will be priests of God and Christ and will reign with him for a thousand years.

So those who will reign with Christ during the thousand years are the martyrs with all those who have not worshipped the beast, nor received the mark on their foreheads and hands. They take part in the first resurrection and they are blessed and holy, but then will not the others take part in the first resurrection? If it is generally claimed that the first resurrection takes place at the time of the rapture of the Church and that the beast will manifest itself later, then why does the apostle John speak of the mark of the beast on people who participate in the first resurrection and who will reign with Christ for a thousand years? Probably, because this mark is not something that will only be part of the great tribulation, but that concerns all believers, even before the rapture!

SATAN FALLING FROM HEAVEN

https://www.christianity.com/theology/theological-faq/how-did-lucifer-fall-and-become-satan-11557519.html

Pope Francis

http://www.newshub.co.nz/home/world/2017/12/satan-is-a-real-person-not-mist-pope-francis.html

89 best Devils Bayou images on pinterest/Demon-Le Baron Samedi.

Paul says that the first resurrection corresponds to the moment when Jesus will return, during what is called the rapture. This is indicated by the following verses:

1 Thessalonians 4:16,17 - "For the Lord himself, at a given signal, at the voice of an archangel, and at the sound of God's trumpet, will come down from heaven, and the dead in Christ will rise first. Then we, the living who have remained, will all be caught up together with them in clouds, to meet the Lord in the air, and so we will always be with the Lord.

http://unimaginablenightmares.blogspot.com

Demonology and dreams: the incubus was a male demon who sought to have relationships with women in their sleep in order to become a father. Some legends describe visiting incubators as a nightmare.

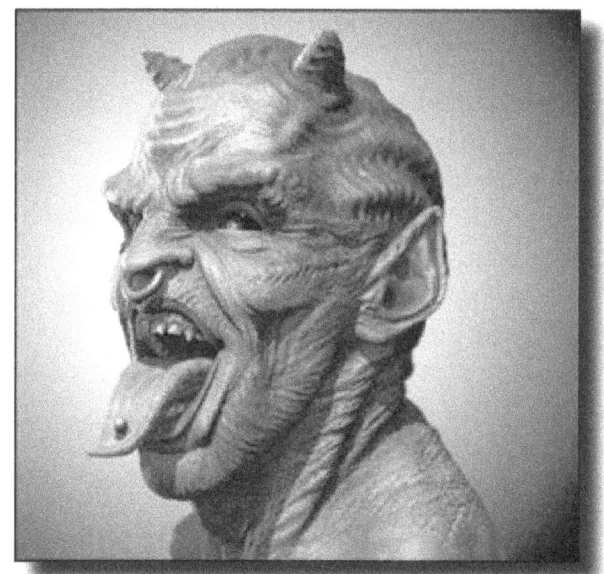

Demon of homosexuality.
http://www.tearstojoyministries.org/

AMERICAN INDIAN DEVIL MONKEY

Frontiers of Zoology: Devil Monkeys Demolish.

Therefore, it is clear that those who come back to life and who did not worship the beast or his image, are not those who remained on earth after the rapture, but rather people who lived before this return of Jesus and before this first resurrection. In this case, those who will reign with Christ for a thousand years will only be martyrs and those who have not taken this mark. The other dead will not come back to life until the thousand years have passed. Will not all of them rise again at the coming of Jesus?

This contradicts what Paul says, because he is not talking about a few dead people but about the dead in Christ, the people we now call the saved. The resurrection is for all those who died in Christ before the coming of Jesus, those who suffered persecution and those who did not take the mark of the beast. It is therefore clear that this mark of the beast cannot be only the reality of a period of the end times, after the rapture of the Church and as a means of salvation for those who have missed the coming of Jesus Christ!

It must be understood that everyone must make the choice to take this brand or not and that this concerns both past and present generations. This mark of the beast has existed since the beginning, it is an obstacle to the respect of God's commandments. We could say that Jesus came to annul the law and that now there is no longer this obstacle. But this is not true, because Jesus himself says that he did not come to abolish it and that even the smallest part of the law will not disappear.

In this regard, the book of Matthew, chapter 5, verses 17 and 18, informs us: "Think not that I have come to abolish the law or the prophets; I have come not to abolish, but to fulfil. For I tell you the truth, until heaven and earth pass away, not a single iota or a single line of letter will disappear from the law until all has happened. »

In this case, the believer must observe the law of the word of God and put it into practice. Unlike the Pharisees, we must follow Christ's example, the way Jesus himself observed his father's law on the basis of love for God and for his neighbor.

Jesus Christ said in Matthew, chapter 22, verses 37-40: "You shall love the Lord your God with all your heart and with all your mind. This is the first and greatest commandment. And here is the second one: you will love your neighbor as yourself. On these two commandments depend all the law and the prophets. He who does not observe my father's rules, who does not put them into practice, this person is no longer guided by God and no longer bears his mark, but bears the mark of man, the 666, working for himself, guided by his own selfishness and leaving aside love for God and for his neighbor.

The believer who does not take this mark of the beast can no longer buy or sell? In a way yes, also today, because when we use the current economic system, we help those who do not love God and who exploit their neighbor. So everyone has the freedom to submit to this system or to refuse it, but I don't think God is asking us to live in a separate world so as not to be contaminated.

Jesus, on the other hand, gave us an example of how to use the system of his time while at the same time manifesting God's values. We must be ready to live in a world that does not respect God's principles, while influencing this world, witnessing to our faith and being ready to suffer persecution. We must reject everything that is contrary to God's will without fear of losing our jobs, without fear of losing our material goods, because they are not our security.

Today, on earth, we are not all facing the same situations, we are not all persecuted. But we all have choices to make in order to respect the values that God asks us to observe, no matter what the cost.

The believers who preceded us did not experience the same events as we do today. But they had to make choices that differentiated them from the values of the world in which they lived. The early Christians were not confronted with the papal inquisition of the Middle Ages, but in their time they had to refuse to worship the Roman emperors in a public and compulsory way.

Others have been subjected to logging, imprisonment or exile. They could no longer do business and were forced to emigrate elsewhere. Even today, many do not receive food aid when they are victims of natural disasters, simply because they are believers. Others are driven from their lands because they do not follow the pagan rituals of their communities.

Each era had its own system of repression with the possibility of denying Jesus in exchange for material benefits. It cannot therefore be said that the decision to bear the mark or reject it will only be valid for those who will live during the great tribulation. Already today, many of our brothers are confronted with such choices. In addition, Jesus said that all those who want to follow Him will be persecuted! So if we are not, it is probably because we have already made compromises with the beast by having an attitude that does not oppose its influence, an attitude where we obey the world more than God's commandments.

It is likely that this smart (or other) system will represent the materialization of a famous mark of the beast at the end of our civilization. But this mark is above all spiritual; each believer must therefore avoid submitting to a system of values that is opposed to God. On the contrary, he will have to submit to God's values and commandments.

The devil, on the other hand, has every interest in making us believe that this brand is purely physical, because he wants to keep us in materialism. He also wants to prevent believers from freeing the oppressed, breaking the chains of wickedness and caring for those in need. For he knows very well that when God's love for the needy is shown, many of them will be touched and will accept Jesus in their lives. The question that is asked of you: of Jesus Christ or of the materialist man, what brand or sign do you choose to take today?

A BIG QUESTION TO ASK HERE: CAN THE DEVIL HEAL THE SICK?

The logical answer would definitely be no, but it may seem different in reality. If the devil makes someone sick, it is quite possible that he can remove the disease he gave. We're not going to talk about a real cure, because it's just an evil taken away by the one who caused it. But on the surface, we will still see a change and therefore a healing. It is therefore quite possible that a preacher, healer or anyone else may give a word of knowledge, identify a person's illness and even free him or her from it. Information and changes thus obtained are due simply to the devil, not to the Holy Spirit.

There are probably many people who heal in this way with the help of the devil; demons make agreements between themselves and, most often, the disease disappears for a while or is exchanged for another.

It is said that a healer would remove the disease from a patient who came to see him, and then pass it on to the next one, from whom he would also remove his disease. Diseases passed from one patient to another and the patient was cured of his illness. But shortly afterwards, he contracted another disease. Since he had already been healed, he would go back to the healer, and the circle would go on forever.

As a Christian, you have to be very careful and know how to behave when you are in places where you talk about healing and miracles. The ideal would be to avoid these places, because some healings could come from demons? YES, just as the existence of counterfeit banknotes does not prevent the use of real ones, counterfeit healings do not prevent there from being real ones too. It is difficult for us to distinguish between the true and the false, but we are called to discern and test the spirits.

1 John, chapter 4, verse 1: "Beloved, do not believe in every spirit; but test the spirits, whether they are of God, for many false prophets have come into the world.

Let us believe in miracles, in healing, but let us do it with discernment, without following men. Let us be guided by Jesus Christ, he is the means to recognize false prophets. Somewhere in the Bible, or precisely in Luke 9:49 and 50, it is said: "Master, we have seen a man casting demons in your name; and we have prevented him from doing so, because he does not follow us. Do not stop him, Jesus answered him; for whoever is not against you is for you.

Let us be vigilant and not follow man, but God. Some people follow men, sometimes they are idolatrous, because they heal, but they do not give glory to God. In this case, even if man follows God, the person who receives healing receives it from man and then from God; his attitude is not good and cannot be blessed.

In any case, I believe in miracles and healing just as I believe in banknotes. At first, I may be fooled by a counterfeit note, but the experience will allow me to recognize them. And if I come across a counterfeit note, I'm not going to use them for any reason either.

Our father loves us, and he will give us good things if we ask him. For he says in Matthew, chapter 7, verses 7 to 11: "Ask, and it will be given to you; seek, and you will find; knock, and it will be opened to you. For whosoever asks receives, he who seeks finds, and it is opened to him who knocks. Which one of you will give a stone to his son if he asks him for bread? Or, if he asks for a fish, will he give him a snake? If then, evil as you are, you know how to give good things to your children, how much more will your father who is in heaven give good things to those who ask him?

WWW.Bible-history.com/past/Dagonenlarged.html.
DAGON- Philistine avenging devil of the sea.

We're going to tell a story about the mark of the Beast, in a way. The first explanation proposed for the meaning of the number 666 is traditionally attributed to Polycarp, the disciple of the apostle John who wrote Revelation. This tradition was preserved in the second (2nd) century in Irenaeus' writings.

The number 666 is contained in Lateinos' Greek letters (see Commentary Of the Whole Bible). Lateinos is a Greek term referring to the Romans. It is interesting to note that the Greek expression, meaning the Latin Kingdom, also has a numerical value of 666. Greek writers commonly called the Roman Empire that way.

The book of Revelation was originally written in Greek, since it was written for churches in ancient Asia Minor. Another interesting explanation involves the name of the emperor Nero, who died twenty-five years before the apostle John wrote Revelation. Although Nero was dead, his reign was nevertheless an image of the Roman system of the late days. He had come to power by promising constitutional reforms and a return to Augustus' golden age, but as his power grew, he became more cruel and despotic.

Living in an atmosphere of intrigue and conspiracy, he abused his power, and was responsible for the first official persecution (of the Roman State) against Christians. During his reign, most of the apostles, including Peter and Paul, were martyred. Its Greek name is Neron Kaesar (Neron Cesar).

When the Greek form of his name is spelled in Hebrew characters, their added numerical values give 666. The founder of ancient Rome was Romulus, from whom the words Rome and Romans derive. In Hebrew, the Latin name Romulus is written
Romiith. In Hebrew, these letters added together make 666. Thus, in both Greek and Hebrew, two languages of the Bible, the number 666 applies to the kingdom derived from Rome.

The next few years will see the seventh and final resurrection of the Holy Roman Empire. There will undoubtedly be a numerical meaning in the name, or perhaps in a special title, of the ruler of times of the end of the power called the beast. Nevertheless, it is important to understand that the Roman system is already marked by the number 666. This system and its final survivor are identified with the beast.

CHAPITRE 14
DUE PROCESS, MAGNA CARTA AND VIOLATION OF HUMANS RIGHTS

THE 5TH AND 14TH CONSTITUTIONAL AMENDMENT OF THE UNITED STATES

A people or a nation that has the privilege of having other nations under his dependence should have known how to dialogue or speak, and be able to know the rights of the citizens of his country and those of other nations. He should also carefully observe the respect for humankind and the Due Process of his country, the United States of America. Everything must be done with respect and in the will of the most high God.

Regular procedure

Due process is the requirement for the State to respect all legal rights that are due to a person. Due process balances the power of the law of the land and protects the individual. When a government hurts a person   without following the exact course of the law, this is a violation of procedure, which contravenes the rule of law.

Due process has often been interpreted as limiting laws and judicial procedures (see substantive procedure) so that judges, instead of legislators, can define and guarantee equity, justice and fundamental freedoms. This interpretation has been controversial.

Like the concepts of natural justice and procedural justice used in various other jurisdictions, the interpretation of due process is sometimes expressed as an order that the government must not be unfair to the people or physically abuse them.

The term is not used in contemporary English law, but two similar concepts are natural justice, which generally applies only to decisions of administrative agencies and certain types of private bodies such as trade unions, and the British constitutional concept of the rule of law as stated by A. V. Dicey and others.

LATIN ENGLISH

Non secundum faciem = Not according to the face
Nolite iudicare secundum faciem sed Iustum iudicium iudicat = Ne jugez pas selon l'apparence, mais jugez selon la justice. Domine non secundum= O us according to our sins.
peccata nostra Faciais nobis
Hoc autem dico secundum = I say this out of condescension indulgentiam don't make them
Non secundum imperiu not an order.

Nihil locutus est mihi et ego non
Secundum vestros sermones respondebo ill.
Denuntiamus autem vobis fratres in nomine Domini nostri jesu christi ut subtrahatis vos ab Omni fratre ambulante inordinate et non secundum Traditionem quam acceperunt a nobi.

Non secundum testamentum quod feci Patribus eorum in die qua adprehendi manum illorum ut Educerem illos de terra Aegypti quoniam ipsi non permanserunt In testamento meo et ego neglexi eos dicit Dominu.
Qui non secundum legem mandati
He did not speak directly to me:
Aussi lui répondrai-je tout other than you.

We recommend to you, brothers, in the name of our Lord Jesus Christ, to distance yourself from any brother who lives in disorder, and not according to the instructions you have received from us.

Not like the alliance I dealt with with their fathers, The day I seize them. By the hand to make them to leave the country of Egypt; for they have not persevered in my Alliance. And I too do not I don't care of them, says the Lord. Established, not under the law of an ordinance Carnalis factus est sed secundum carnal, but according to the power of an imperishable life; Virtutem vitae insolubili Qui nos liberavit et vocavit vocatione sancta non secundum opera nostra sed secundum propositum suum et gratiam quae data est nobis in Christo Jesu ante tempora saeculari Par la puissance de Dieu qui nous a sauvés, et nous a adressé une sainte vocation, non à cause de nos œuvres, mais selon la grâce qui nous a été donnée en Jésus-Christ avant les temps éternels.

Si ergo consummmatio per sacerdotium leviticum erat populus enim sub ipso legem accepit quid adhuc necessarium secundum ordinem Melchisedech alium surgere sacerdotem et non secundumordinem Aaron dic = If then perfection had been possible through the Levitical priesthood, for it is on this priesthood that the law given to the people is based, what else was it necessary that there should be another priest according to the order of Melchizedek, and not according to the order of Aaron?

Ut iustificatio legis impleretur in nobis qui non secundum carnem ambulamus sed secundum Spiritu = And this that the righteousness of the law might be fulfilled in us, who walk, not according to the flesh, but according to the spirit.

Et replebit eum spiritus timoris Domini non secundum visionem oculorum iudicabit neque secundum auditum aurium argue = He will breathe the fear of the Lord; he will not pronounce himself on a hearsay.

Et scietis quia ego Dominus cum benefecero vobis propter nomen meum non secundum vias vestras malas neque secundum scelera vestra pessima domus Israhel ait Dominus Deus = And you will know that I am the Lord, when I act with you for my name's sake, and not according to your evil conduct and your corrupt deeds, O house of Israel, says the Lord God.

Non secundum pactum quod pepigi cum patribus vestris in die qua adprehendi manum eorum ut educerem eos de terra Aegypti pactum quod irritum fecerunt et ego dominatus sum eorum dicit Dominus = Not as the covenant that I made with their fathers in the day that I took them by the hand to bring them out of the land of Egypt, which they broke, even though I was their master, says the Lord.

MAGNA CARTA

In clause 39 of the Magna Carta, issued in 1215, John of England promised: No free man shall be seized or imprisoned, or stripped of his rights or possessions, or proscribed or exiled, or otherwise deprived of his position, nor shall we pursue with force against him, or send others to do so, except by the legal judgment of his equals or by the law of the land.

Magna Carta itself immediately became part of the law of the land, and Article 61 of this charter authorized an elected body of 25 barons to determine by majority vote W reparation hat the king must provide when the king offends "in all respect against a man. "Thus, Magna Carta established the rule of law in England by requiring the monarchy not only to obey the law of the land, but also to limit how it could change the law from which it lands. However, in the thirteenth century, these provisions may have referred only to the rights of landowners, not to ordinary peasants or villagers, etc.

A CREATOR WHO HAS NOT BEEN CREATED

The biblical story of creation is based on the fact that there is a supreme being, the Almighty God, who created all things. Who is he? Who is he? What is he like?

The Bible reveals that he is very different from the divinities described in popular culture and traditional religions. He is the creator of all things, yet most people know very little about him.

God is a person. It is not an indefinite force without any personality, which wanders aimlessly in the universe. God has thoughts, feelings and goals. God has infinite power and wisdom. Hence the complex mechanisms and forms that can be found everywhere in nature, especially in living things. God created all matter. It cannot be made of physical elements that he himself has manufactured. God is of a spiritual, immaterial nature.

God does not have a time-limited existence. It has always existed and will always exist. It was therefore not created. God has a name of his own that is used thousands of times in the Bible. That name is the Lord God. The Lord God loves and cares for humans.

How long did it take God to create the universe?
The Bible states that God created the heavens and the earth. This statement, which is very general, gives no indication of how long it took to create the universe or how it was done.

What about the idea spread by creationists that God created the universe in six 24-hour days? This idea, largely rejected by scientists, is based on a misinterpretation of the biblical account. The Bible often uses the term day to refer to various periods of time. Sometimes the length of these periods is not specified. This is the case for the account of creation reported in the book of Genesis.

In the biblical account, each day of creation could have lasted thousands of years. When the first day of creation began, God had already created the universe, including the earth, where there was still no life. The six days of creation were, it seems, long periods during which the Lord God arranged the earth so that it could receive humans.

Has God used evolution? Many who do not believe in the Bible accept the theory that living beings came into existence through unknown and blind processes, based on inanimate chemical elements. They think that at some point, a self-replicating organism, such as a bacterium, appeared and gradually diversified to give all the species that exist today.

Thus, the human being, in all its complexity, would in fact come from a bacterium. The theory of evolution is accepted by many people who say they believe in the Bible. They believe that God produced the first spark of life on earth, and then simply monitored, or even guided, the process of evolution. But that's not what the Bible teaches. According to the Bible, God the Almighty created all the great groups of plants and animals. He also created a perfect man and woman, possessing self-awareness, and capable of love, wisdom and justice.

The animals and plants created by God have obviously undergone changes that have produced variations within each group. The resulting life forms are often very different from each other. The biblical account of creation does not exclude that there may be variations within groups of animals and plants, as scientists observe.

WHO MADE GOD?

Many arguments claiming to demonstrate the existence of God have been put forward over the centuries. Yet the answer to some of these arguments is: if God created the universe, who created God? This suggests that arguments in favour of God's existence only push the question of origins back a notch. The Bible, the word of God, and Christian doctrine answer this question by affirming that God is eternal and uncreated, but such an answer rarely satisfies unbelievers.

A philosophical response is to consider God as the root cause; atheism must face the dilemma of what or from whom this root cause might well be. An uncreated creator may ultimately be a more plausible explanation of the universe in which we live. Our universe seems to have a beginning, and to be well adapted for the appearance of life, giving a place for love and purpose.

GOD CREATED HUMANITY IN PERFECT HARMONY.

What will happen to someone who is biased and racist? Can we escape stereotypes and prejudices?

THE ORIGIN OF PREJUDICES

The Larousse dictionary defines prejudice as a judgment on someone, or something, formed in advance according to certain personal criteria. A prejudice is an idea accepted without demonstration, just like an axiom or postulate. However, if prejudice is considered by the person who adheres to it as a truth, the axiom or postulate is based on philosophical or scientific thought, and is seen as a working hypothesis that can be used independently of any assessment of its truthful nature.

It is important to differentiate between certain notions sometimes associated with prejudice, such as stereotyping and discrimination. A prejudice is a feeling. It is a preliminary judgment on a person or group of persons, without sufficient knowledge to assess the situation.

The stereotype, on which prejudice is based, is a generalization, a set of mental images that influence our relationship to reality. Finally, these two concepts must be distinguished from discrimination, which corresponds to behavior, an act induced by prejudice.

It should be noted that prejudice has two essential aspects. The first corresponds to the capacity of prejudices across time and generations without undergoing very significant changes. The second refers to the simplifying and globalizing characteristic of prejudice, insofar as each category of person (e. g. particular professions, gender, etc.) is associated with a limited set of specific attributes that are supposed to refer to a kind of essence, an intrinsic nature. The non-questioning of an individual's prejudices and opinions is a factor of ignorance.

SHOULD NOT BE CONFUSED WITH PREJUDICE.

The term prejudice (prior judgment) refers to opinions adopted in the absence of sufficient information or practice. Sometimes, articulated on myths or beliefs, or resulting from early generalization, prejudices are considered from a Bayesian perspective as the starting point for any acquisition of information, the learning process consisting simply in correcting them as quickly as possible in the light of experience.

RACISM.

Racism is an ideology that, starting from the premise that races exist within the human species, considers that certain categories of people are inherently superior to others.

This ideology can lead to a systematic attitude of hostility or sympathy towards a specific category of people. This hostility towards another cultural and ethnic group is reflected in forms of xenophobia or ethnocentrism. Some forms of expression of racism, such as racist insults, racial defamation and discrimination, are considered crimes in a number of countries. Racist ideologies have served as the basis for political doctrines leading to racial discrimination, ethnic segregation and injustices and violence, including genocide.

CHAPTER 15
POLITICAL DOCTRINES

I want to remind you that I am not only a preacher, a pastor or theologian who has been preaching the Gospel of Jesus Christ for 37 years.

I hold an Associate of Arts paralegal degree (or attorney), a Bachelor of liberal studies or legal studies (always law). I am a juris doctor candidate in law, i.e. a candidate lawyer who waits for the exams to obtain the law degree. I also have a degree in business administration .As a graduate in several fields, I would like to share with you some instructions in the following subjects: finance, law, political science, etc. I studied political science at university, and I am a politician because of my studies in politics, but I don't do the practice.

CPA.

The CPA is a Certified Public Accountant (CPA) who has received training at a university recognized by the U.S. federal government. This certification is considered a decisive step. Once the official tests have been passed, you become a CPA, i.e. a certified accountant.

MBA

The Master of Business Administration (MBA) is a generalized study in the field of business, marketing, leadership, etc. It can be extended to different areas: hospital, education, hotel, airport, airline, store opening, car and tire sales, etc. Anything can be done, depending on the area of specialization: accounting, finance, marketing, human resources, management operations, strategy, etc.

It can be said that the MBA curriculum is not limited to economics, marketing or organizational behavior. If you have an MBA, you have a wide range of possibilities. You can work in a management department, be a marketing manager, investment banker, financial advisor, etc.

On the other hand, location plays a major role in the remuneration of the MBA holder. Overall, the MBAs and professional master's degrees in the Faculty of Business Administration are designed to strengthen your knowledge, analytical skills and critical thinking skills to enhance your ability to make complex business decisions. In addition to developing your management skills, they prepare you to work in a globalized world. They also aim to make you an ethical, socially responsible manager or analyst with leadership and communication skills.

While you may start in entry-level positions, there is potential to reach high-level management jobs in the business world - including CFO, CEO, or even business owner:

Job Title

Salary for experienced professional

HR DIRECTOR	$124,942
Financial controller	$121,361
Operation Manager	$91,016
HR Manager	$89,615
Executive Assistant	$77,281
Office Manager	$67,133

Job and salary data provided by the U.S. Bureau of Labor Statistics.

The above table highlights the U.S. Bureau of Labor Statistics high salary range for several career specializations for individuals attaining a Bachelor's degree in Business Administration, and the numbers are impressive

Common Business Administration concentrations include: HUMAN RESSOURCES FINANCE MARKETING MANAGEMENT HEALTH SERVICES ADMINISTRATION HOSPITALITY AND TOURISM

There are several areas of Business Administration that you can pursue, and your choice depends on your skill-set and interests.

INTRODUCTION TO POLITICAL SCIENCE.

This teaching approaches political science through the fundamental concepts of power. It situates the discipline, its ancient and recent history, as well as its epistemological foundations. Then he deepens cardinal notions (power, politics, the State), and presents the main political regimes such as democracy, totalitarianism and authoritarianism. At each of these stages, in a pedagogical view, the reflection articulates elements from history, sociology, philosophy, law and anthropology. The course thus provides an introduction to some of the major works in the social sciences.

The objective of the Political Science course is to study the main systems that concern political science, namely the state, political regimes, political forces, political participation, elites, public policies.

Political science is the science that studies political phenomena. More precisely, it consists in studying political processes involving power relations between individuals, groups, and especially within the State.

Political science studies objects traditionally perceived as political, the state, governmental or parliamentary institutions, public decisions, elections, political parties, political doctrines and ideologies, international relations, etc.

Political science also studies, from a sociological perspective, the politicized dimension of social relations: relations between classes or communities, phenomena of social domination, links between economic life and the political system, between social inequalities and political participation, between religious affiliation and political activities, etc.

JUDICIAL PROCEDURE, CIVIL PROCEDURE, ARBITRATION, ETC.

Civil procedure is the set of formulas that enable the holder of a right to enforce his prerogatives by resorting to the courts of civil order. Civil proceedings, the necessary extension of which is carried out by means of enforcement, concern all the rules concerning the organization of justice and its functioning. It brings together individuals (legal or natural persons) who are in principle in charge of the trial. The purpose of the civil procedure course is to study the characteristics of civil procedure, the fundamental principles of civil procedure, its conduct before the courts of general and special jurisdiction and the respective roles of the judicial judge and the parties to the proceedings throughout the civil proceedings.

As a first step, it is necessary to define the concept of procedure. This is constituted by all the rules of law, according to which the trial is organized, and according to which a dispute may be submitted to a court.

Civil procedure is the procedure applicable before the courts of law, competent for all disputes under private law, involving exclusively individuals. It is thus opposed to criminal procedure, which is the one applied before the criminal courts. It is also opposed to administrative litigation, which concerns appeals to administrative courts.

It can be said that the current regime of civil procedure has its source in the former Code of Civil Procedure. However, it has not known the durability of the Civil Code. One of its major disadvantages was that it was too much based on the old 1667 ordinance. Many amendments were made and led to the drafting of the new Code of Civil Procedure in 1975, to which were added other amendments by means of decrees.

American law is based on two key ideas: it is a federal system in which the constitution has established mechanisms for balance or self-regulation. There is a federal state of the U.S.A. that coexists with 50 other states. We will have to think on two levels, but we must be aware that each American state has its own rules of law and jurisdictions.

There is a federal constitution, adopted in 1787, that sets out rules for each state, but Texas, for example, has its own law in addition to federal law. The law of Texas is governed by the Constitution of Texas.

We also have a federal judicial system with federal courts, i.e. a federal court responsible for handling federal cases, the last level of jurisdiction being the Supreme Court of the United States.

The legislative power is the Congress, which is the equivalent of our parliament. It is composed of two chambers: the Senate and the House of Representatives. What are they used for? They will pass legislation. It is often the President of the United States who takes the initiative and it is the legislative power that adopts and votes on laws. We are in a democratic conception of the law; the powers are separate.

The second power is responsible for enforcing the law, for applying it: it is the executive power. The President of the United States, who holds this power, is elected for a term of 4 years and can be re-elected for 4 years, but no more. There is no government, but to fulfil his mission, the American president is accompanied by a team called the administration: it is the president's office. They are a kind of minister, at the head of individual administrations.

The third power is the judiciary, the power of judges. Judges in the United States do much more than settle disputes. The Supreme Court, in particular, has a role to play

much more important: it is the guardian of the constitution. In disputes before it, he may ask questions of application, not only of the law, but also of the constitution. Can a person be incarcerated for two years have the right to see their lawyers? These are the types of issues that the Federal Supreme Court often has the opportunity to decide.

GUIDE TO CRIMINAL PROSECUTION IN THE UNITED STATES

As a citizen living in America, and as a man of law, I think that everyone here should know their rights. Why? Why? Because there is too much sabotage on the citizens living in this country. There is not enough respect for human rights. Students are periodically attacked in their schools and even on the streets. Parents send their children to school and do not have the chance to see them return home. These are painful situations, and we are all saddened on such a occasion. Fortunately, Jesus Christ will come back to put an end to these kinds of problems.

Introduction to practices and procedures

In the United States, the federal government, like the states, has the authority to initiate criminal proceedings. The federal government and the states have their own criminal statutes, their own court systems, their own prosecutors, and their own police organizations.

Whether it is a specific crime that can be prosecuted by a state or the federal government, too many and complex factors should be taken into account to be considered in this brief presentation. By virtue of both legal and practical factors, the crimes most frequently prosecuted are drug trafficking, organized crime, financial crimes, large-scale fraud, crimes of particular federal interest and fraud against the United States.

In addition, there are certain crimes that can only be prosecuted by the federal government. These include customs crimes, tax crimes, and crimes of espionage and treason.

The United States prosecutes crimes against persons, such as murder, attacks and various property offences such as burglaries and robberies. In fact, state courts have jurisdiction over a wider variety of disputes than federal courts.

Although States have a broad authority to exercise jurisdiction over a wide range of offences, they are empowered to initiate investigations and criminal proceedings only for crimes committed within their borders. The jurisdiction of the federal government, on the other hand, extends throughout the territory of the United States. As a result, the federal government is often in a better position to investigate and prosecute more sophisticated and large-scale criminal activities.

The Office of International Affairs ("OIA"), Criminal Affairs Division, of the United States Department of Justice, is responsible for all criminal matters, extraditions, and international legal assistance for both state and federal prosecutors. In this capacity, the OIA oversees the representation of extradition and evidence requests from foreign governments before the courts of the United States.

Although there are differences in criminal procedures between States, and between States and the federal government, certain fundamental principles of United States criminal law and related practices apply to investigations and prosecutions at both the state and federal levels. First of all, it should be stressed that throughout the United States, investigations and prosecutions of crimes are the responsibility of the executive branch. Prosecutors, investigators, and police officers are members of the executive, not the judiciary. In the United States, the concept of the investigating judge does not exist, unlike the civil law system.

As a result, the role of judges in the investigation of offences is limited. However, some measures may only be taken during an investigation with the authorization of the judge. Only a judge can issue a warrant to search and seize evidence of an offence; only a judge can give an order to wiretap; only a judge can take steps to enforce a summons to appear or face a fine. For a witness to give evidence, or produce documents or other evidence in his or her possession, under penalty of incarceration if refused and, except in limited circumstances, only a judge may issue an arrest warrant against an accused person.

When a prosecutor (for us, in some cases, a police officer) determines that such legal action is necessary to conduct an investigation, he or she must submit a formal request to the court, and present facts or evidence that they are sufficient under the law to support the required action. A judge will only issue a warrant or order if he or she determines that the evidence presented is sufficient to establish the probable cause to believe that an offence has been committed, and that the evidence of that offence resides in a specific place that must be searched.

Secondly, certain aspects of the procedure in criminal cases are required under the United States Constitution. These apply to prosecutions at both the state and federal levels. For example, a person accused of a serious offence has the right to be tried by jury and to have legal advice. During his or her trial, the defendant has the right to question the persons who testify against him or her. Similarly, the Constitution requires that no warrant be issued until it has been determined that there is sufficient evidence to support probable cause.

Therefore, an arrest warrant can only be issued until there is sufficient evidence to support the argument that it is much more likely that an offence has been committed, and that the person to be arrested has committed the offence.

With regard to BLACK'S LAW DICTIONARY: this book contains very informative legal terms for people interested in the law.

For example:
Aider by pleading over: The cure of a pleading defect by an adversary's answering the pleading without an objection, so that the objection is waived.

Help by verdict. The cure of a pleading defect by a trial verdict, based on the presumption that the record contains adequate proof of the necessary facts even if those facts were not specifically alleged.

Also termed cure by verdict.
Abettor: A person who aids, encourages, or assists in the commission of a crime. Also spelled a better.
See principal in the second degree under principal.

Ability: The capacity to perform an act or service; exp. The power to carry out a legal act, ability to enter into a contract.

Abjudge (ab-jej) , Archaic . To take away or remove (something) by judicial decision.

Abjuration (ab-juu-ray-shen) ., n. A renouncing by oath. Abjuration of the realm: An oath taken to leave the realm forever.

Abjure (ab-joor), to renounce formally or on oath < abjure one's citizenship > To avoid or abstain from < abjure one's civic duties >.-

Abjuratory (abjoor -e-toree), adj. Able to work: Labor law . (Of a worker) released from medical care and capable of employment; Esp. , not qualified to receive unemployment benefits on grounds of illness or injury.

Abolish, vb. To annul, eliminate, or destroy , esp . an ongoing practice or thing.

Abolition .1- The act of abolishing. 2- The state of being annulled or abrogated. 3. usu .cap .) The legal termination of slavery in the United States. 4. Civil law. Withdrawal of a criminal accusation ; a sovereign's remission of punishment for a crime. 5.

Hist. . permission granted to the accuser in a criminal action to withdraw from its prosecution.

Absentee , n. 1 . A person who is away from his or her usual residence; one who is absent-2. A person who is not present where expected . 3. A person who either resides out of state or has departed from the state without having a representative there.

Absolute-bar rule .The principle that, when a creditor sells collateral without giving reasonable notice to the debtor, the creditor may not obtain a deficiency judgment for any amount of the debt that is not satisfied by the sale.

Absolute disparity: Constitutional law, The difference between the percentage of a group in the general population and the percentage of that group in the pool of prospective jurors on a venire. For example, if African-American makes up 12 % of a country's population and 8

% of the potential jurors on a venire, the absolute disparity of African-American venire-members is 4%. The reason for calculating the disparity is to analyze a claim that the jury was not impartial because the venire from which it was chosen did not represent a fair cross-section of the jurisdiction's population. Some courts criticize the absolute- disparity analysis, in the belief that the deviation.

Absolute-priority rule: Bankruptcy. The rule that a confirmable reorganization plan must provide for full payment to a class of dissenting unsecured creditors before a junior class of claimants will be allowed to receive or retain anything under the plan. Some jurisdictions recognize an exception to this rule when a junior class member, usu. a partner or shareholder of the debtor, contributes new capital in exchange for an interest in the debtor.

Absorbable. n . The act or process of including or incorporating a thing into something else; esp. , the application of rights guaranteed by U.S. Constitution to actions by the states . 2. Int'l law . the merger of one nation into another, whether voluntarily or by subjugation . 3. Labor law . In a post merger collective-bargaining agreement, a provision allowing seniority for union members in the resulting entity. 4. Real estate. The rate at which property will be leased or sold on the market at a given time. 5. Commercial law. A sales method by which a manufacturer pays the reseller's freight costs , which the manufacturer accounts for before quoting the reseller a price. Also termed (in sense 5) freight absorption.

Executive: N. 1- The branch of government responsible for effecting and enforcing laws; the person or persons who constitute this branch. The executive branch is sometimes said to be the residue of all government after subtracting the judicial and legislative branches. Sometimes also termed executive department.

Chief executive. The head of the executive branch of government, such as the president of the United States. A corporate officer at the upper levels of management. Also termed executive officer; executive employee .- Executive , adj.

Executive Administration. Collectively, high public officials who administer the chief department of the government.

Executive Agency. An executive-branch department whose activities are subject to statute and whose contracts are subject to judicial review. One example is the National Aeronautics and space Agency.

Executive Agreement. An international agreement entered into by the president, without approval by the Senate, and us . involving routine diplomatic or military matters.

Executive branch. The branch of government charged with administering and carrying out the law.

Executive employee. An employee whose duties include some form of managerial authority and active participation in the control, supervision, and management of the business, often shortened to executive.

TORTS-LAW
INDEPENDENT CONTRACTORS.
DEFINITION:

An independent contractor is one who:

A- Is engaged to perform a certain service for another according to his own methods and manner;

And

B- Is free from control and direction of his employer in all matters connected with the performance of the service except as to the results.

2-GENERAL RULES:

The employer is not liable for the torts of independent contractors.

2- Exceptions

A- The independent contractor is engaged in inherently dangerous activities ., or

B- The duty, because of public policy considerations, is non delegable. (Suing the city ? yes !)

D-Employer may be directly liable for:

Negligent hiring (independent contractor - negligent selection , or retention, Negligent training, and Negligent supervision.

E- JOINT ENTERPRISE:

When two people are in a business venture and have a common purpose and mutual right of control, then each may be vicariously liable for the tortious acts committed by the other as long as the tort is committed within the scope of that venture is (husband & wife) partnership : when two People are in a business for profit, then each may be vicariously liable for the tortious acts committed by the other partner as long as the torts is committed within the scope of the partnership .

F- HUSBAND & WIFE

1- COMMON LAW :

A husband was liable for the torts of his wife.

Modernly: A spouse is not liable for the torts of his / her spouse. Parent for Minor child.

COMMON LAW : a parent is not vicariously liable for the torts of their child.

Modernly; most states, by State, make parents liable for the intentional torts of their minor children up to a certain dollar amount. Imputed contributory Negligence.

CRIMINAL LAW

1- CLASSIFICATION OF CRIMES

A- FELONY
INCARCERATION MORE THAN 1 YEAR
TIME IS SERVED IN PRISON

B- MISDEMEANOR STOP SIGN -LICENSE EXPIRED
INCARCERATION UP 1 YEAR.
TIME IS SERVED IN JAIL

C- INFRACTION - TICKET FOR SPEEDING STOP SIGN
NO POSSIBLE NO RIGHT TO JURY TRIAL

2- NO RIGHT TO COURT APPOINTED, FELONEY OR MISDEMEANOR –ATTORNEY

NOTICE TO BUYERS AND READERS

We ask everyone to pay close attention to this book.

This book is written for a specific purpose, just to organize a fundraising event to rebuild "Saint Heirloom International University".

We have a great dream for this Haitian, American and other community. We would like to take this opportunity to inform you that the university to which we referred will be opened shortly. We hope that everything will be done in order, by the grace of Almighty God.

We also encourage you to take part in this great project, and to help us for the good functioning of the community of Orlando and that of the other States.

We are convinced that the Lord will open the necessary doors for this great vision so long cherished.

Thank you! Thank you!

May the Lord, the great Almighty God, bless you all richly!

Dr. Raymond Saintil, the author of this book.

CONCLUSION

All what has just been said is indisputable and certain.

However, those who rule over nations do not see that these ignominies inevitably bring the end of the world. No, they don't realize it, they have no idea and have no idea. They believe that this world is their own world, built according to their points of view, convinced that they will always dominate without there ever being an end.

Blind and unaware of the disaster, they do not know what they are saying or doing.

They do not see where they are leading nations, because they are not lucid enough to know that the end of the world is the logical outcome of their mistakes. Having never read the Scriptures that openly condemn them, they give free rein to their desires for glory and power, making them presumptuous, blind, deaf, arrogant and destructive.

But for you who see the deplorable state of this world, it is not enough to understand that this end cannot be avoided or postponed. No, you have to know why the world is coming to an end, and that there will be another world right after this corrupt world. To do this, we must download and read this book of the Holy Prophet who predicts for our difficult times.

Patiently, he leads us into all the truth, showing why the world is suffering more and more. He exhorts us to prepare ourselves to face this inevitable end of the world (according to Revelation) so that it will only make the unjust ones disappear (the goats and pigs in writing), those who respect nothing.

After that, a better world without authority, without power, without domination, without exploitation of man, and very well defined by the Lamb and the law, will replace it according to prophecy.

Dr. Raymond Saintil

Founder of HEADQUARTERS OF Mission HOPE GLOBAL VISION. - EL CUARTEL DE LA MISION ESPERANZA VISION MUNDIAL)(A BAPTIST BELIEF) (founded in 1993)
Address: 624 Wilks Avenue, Orlando, Florida 32809.
Téléphone : 407- 438-3162 (Cell.)
E-mail address : revraymo541@yahoo.com

QUALIFICATIONS

18 YEARS in secondary school education from the third class to high school diploma.

Modern languages, Castellano or Spanish, English, accountant graduated from Gérard Armand Joseph's business college.

Studied at the Lope de Vega Institute, and the Haitian-American Institute, Port-au-Prince, Haiti.

PROFESSIONS:

Group home, Certified Nursing Assistant . 1990-2000.
Certified Day care center of Florida -- C D L (commercial driver license).

Paralegal, CEO Of Terrae Filius paralegal & multi-services - Orlando,FL. -2006 -2011.
CHAPLAIN NATIONAL & INTERNATIONAL ,
UNIVERSITIES :

KEISER UNIVERSITY, ORLANDO, FL.
BARRY UNIVERSITY, ORLANDO,FL.
NOVA SOUTHEASTERN UNIVERSITY, ORLANDO, FL.

AMERICAN HERITAGE UNIVERSITY SCHOOL OF LAW, LOS ANGELES, CALIFORNIA.J.D. , Candidate ,

M.B.A. , general Busines : EVERGLADES UNIVERSITY, MAITLAND, FL. NORTH CENTRAL UNIVERSITY , PH.D. B.A. , ARIZONA, U.S.A.

What is the best definition of a Christian? When can we say that we are Christians? A Christian is one who believes in Jesus Christ, that is, who recognizes Him as Savior and Lord.

This language may seem quite religious. Let's go into more detail. A Christian is not simply someone who was baptized when he was a child, or who received a Christian education, in which case we will speak of a sociological Christian. This one is of Christian culture, but is not really Christian, because he does not adhere to the confession of Christian faith, and has no real, concrete relationship with Christ.

Being a Christian is a choice. A Christian is someone who has personally appropriated the faith and lives a living and true relationship with God. This personal appropriation of the faith is precisely called conversion. Conversion, as we have said, can be brutal, dramatic, instantaneous. But it can also be progressive, spread over time; as the result of a thoughtful and assumed assimilation of a Christian education.

One can also become a Christian because one has heard the message of the Gospel. We understood it and we adhered to it with all our being, by committing our intelligence, our will, our feelings, etc. A Christian is therefore one who recognizes in Jesus his savior, who relies on him for his salvation, for the forgiveness of his sins, for his entire life. He is the one whose life has been enlightened by the light of the Gospel, transformed and restored. He received new life from God.

The apostle Paul said: "If anyone is in Christ, he is a new creature. The old things have passed away; behold, all things have become new" (2 Cor. 5:17). A Christian is also someone who wants to live as a consistent disciple of Christ. This means that he is an apprentice at the school of Christ. He's trying to live the ethics of the Kingdom and the values of the Gospel. He is concerned about sanctification, reflecting Christ, glorifying God in all areas of his life.

1 CORINTHIANS 12: THE CHURCH IS THE BODY OF CHRIST. "May the peace established by Christ govern your decisions. For it is to this peace that God has called you to form one body. And be grateful" (from Colossians 3:15).

Be grateful for the Church? This is already an important awareness. What about all the members of this body? It is made up of different members; some seem essential, others less so. In the Church, some people are important; they take an active part in material and spiritual life; they have been or are committed to the Church's council, are monitors, speak in worship. And there are others, people who are not often heard, who are not noticed; and for some of them, their place in the Church is like the one you can occupy in worship: at the bottom. But don't think I'm saying it to criticize.

ON WHICH ROCK DID CHRIST BUILD HIS CHURCH?

A large church claims that its authority is based on the premise that Jesus founded his church on the apostle Peter. Was Peter the rock to which Christ referred ? Verse 18 of Matthew 16 gives exactly the passage of the scripture used to claim that the apostle Peter and those who are considered to be his successors have received almost unlimited spiritual authority. What did Christ say? Jesus had just asked his disciples a question: "Who do you think I am, the son of man?" (Verse 13). Peter had answered first, incidentally giving the right answer to verse 16. But instead of congratulating Peter on his correct answer, Jesus spoke of stones.

"I tell you that you are a stone, and that on this rock I will build my church, and that the gates of She shall not prevail against it" (verse 18). Jesus spoke of Peter, stones, his Church, and the gates of She (hades); a statement certainly full of meaning! What exactly did he want to talk about? Petra, which means the word that Peter has just spoken, that is, touched by the Holy Spirit.

ABOUT THE AUTHOR

Dr. Raymond Saintil has accepted Jesus Christ as his personal savior since the age of 13. While born into a Christian family, Christ chose him from his mother's womb to become a spokesman and servant for nations throughout the world. Through his ministry, many sick people have been able to find a cure. Their Christian lives have improved. People are married and educated in different ways. And it is also there to educate people at university and other levels. Already in Haiti, he was serving the community. Eighteen years in education, and twenty-three years at the religious level! This means that his entire life will be dedicated to ministry on both the social and educational levels, for the glory of God . He is also vested with the tremendous power of God's Holy Spirit to write sacred books that speak of the upcoming return of our Savior and Lord Jesus Christ. He also has the power to pray for everyone, whatever the circumstances.

That's why he encourages you to read this book on a weekly basis.

REFERENCES

Bible Texts on Couples and Marriage - Genesis- Chapter 1

Proverbs - Chapter 31 - Psalms 127 - Song of Songs.

Gospel according to St. Mark, Chapter 10 - Gospel according to Saint John - Chapter 2.

First letter of Saint Paul to the Corinthians - Chapter 13.

Letter of Saint Paul to the Ephesians - Chapter 5 - Colossians - Chapter 3.

Letter to the Hebrews - Chapter 13 – First letter to Saint Peter - Chapter 3

Louis Segond Bible - The Holy Bible --- Detailed Bible study, Genesis chapter 1 - 11

The Creation: Genesis 1 - Free Genesis Bible Course . Dallas Theological Seminary.

The submission of the wife to the husband - in Ephesians 5 - wise advice for couples on which rock did Christ build his church? (Matth. 16:18)

True Couple Love: How to know if it is love or usually?

The concept of love -

The last enemy to be destroyed is death. --- The Holy Bible.

The English Online Bible (FRN 97) -- First Letter to Corinthians 15 .

The relations between parents and children - Epistle to the Ephesians. - Proverbs 23:13 - Do not spare the child correction - Louis Segond Bible. - 5 Tips for better communicating with young children.

Psychomedia - - History of Christian Theology in the Apostolic Century.

Transform your home into a haven of peace: one guide room by room.

Readings Weddings . WWW. Parish-moutiers, fr./--./ - Choice of readings - Bibles .

Marriage and Divorce - Parpaillot. Free.fr./erl-est/ preaching / divorce. doc.

1-The institution of Marriage - 2- The nature of Marriage -3- Marriage, family, Society and Church.

The best tips and advice for a happy and lasting marriage.

The five senses: The Touch. -Love / Define Love at Dictionary.com.

7 Principles to make your love last. -Bad conceptions or attitudes of prayer.

How to get an answer to your prayers? chapter 10 - Why are there so many blockages in the Christian home? - Is Christ divided in their married life (chapter 11).

The Lord is tired of the world and would like to turn his back on it (chap. 12).

Voodoo --- The Last Judgment - Rev. 20 : 2 . ---Even nature revolts - chap. 13.

Due Process - - -Magna Carta - https://.bing.com/search ?q=translate&qsLS&pq=tra&sk. and

violation of rights -chap.14 - How to build a happy marriage?

Wex Legal Dictionary / Encyclopedia/ l'" /Legal .--- A creator who has not been created.

Who made God? - God created humanity in perfect harmony. - The origin of prejudice.

Racism. -5 Ways to feed the woman. Welcoming, spirituality - Israel - Present. In front of Christ's court, what will happen? Who made God? If God created the universe, who created God?

Criminal-law--- Classification of Crimes -Blacks-law-Dictionary - Guide to Criminal Prosecutions in the United States -TORTS-LAW -Common-law --Independent contractors -

Husband was liable for the Torts of his wife.

What is the best definition of a Christian? The Church, the Body of Christ - Audio preaching.

IMAGE REFERENCES

1. https:// hellhorror.com/demon.name-598/succubus.htm/
2. pope Francis-https:// Chicago.suntimes.com/opinion/ married-catholic-priests.
3. Partners in Ministry- www.gmp777.net/f.why is taking-666 markofbeast-so wrong.htm/ Godsmasterplan.Satan's throne-At the Vatican.
4. Anti-christ philistine god of the sea American Indian devil monkey- Dagon the Fish God enlarged-www.Bible-history. com/past/ dagonenlarged.html
5. Frontiers of Zoology: Devil Monkeys Demolish-
6. Dagon-Damballa - 89 best Devils Bayou images on pinterest/ Demon-Le Baron Samedi.
7. Inccubus -http:// unimaginablenightmares.blogspot. com/2015/12/ incubus-andsuccubus.html
8. Demon of homosexuality-www.tearstojoyministries.org
9. Pope-www.newshub.co.nz/home/world/2027/satan is a real-person-not- mist-pope-francis.html
10. Satan falling from heaven -www.christianity.com/theology/ theological faq/how-did-lucifer-fall&become -satan11557519. html
11. https://st.lucifer666.bandcamp.com/releases
12. http://www.ncregister.com/daily-news/pope-francis-first-easter.

BIOGRAPHY

I was ordained pastor in Port-au-Prince, Haiti, in 1984 by the Montagne de L'Eternel mission. That same year, I was sworn in at the Department of Worship and the Courthouse in Port-au-Prince.

I am the founder of the first Baptist Church of Moussignac , Miragoane, Haiti, around 1978-1984, and I received a certification from the Red Cross. Then I received another ordination and a license from Florida Baptist Convention, for the operation of the church in the United States. And I am the founder, in 1993, of the Mission of the Haitian Baptist Church of Bethany, whose address is as follows: 624 wilks Avenue, Orlando, Florida 32809.

After careful consideration, I decided to deepen my knowledge at American universities in order to be able to offer education to adults and young people in the Haitian community and others.

I am also the founder and president of the Central Florida Evangelical Leaders Unit (Pastors' Association).
Teaching experiences :
Post secondary: teaching languages Port-au-prince -Haiti.
Jonas Augustin College
Martin Luther king College
Saint-Yves College
Louis -Mercier College
Brother Pierre Louis College
Heart Of Jesus College
Amedee College Brown
Oswald Durand College
Frère Raymond Saintil College 1976-1985
Haitian American Institute -P-AU-P-Haiti- English Review by the department of Education

Graduated from Gerard Armand Joseph College of Commerce-Accounting 1982 -Citizenship Bible

College -Haiti - 1977 Attended linguistic school of LOPE DE VEGA, Bois-Verna , P-AU-P . Haiti . LAW SCHOOL: American Heritage University school of Law, U.S.A. California -J.D. CANDIDATE .

Keiser University - Orlando, Florida - Associate of paralegal -U.S.A. year of Graduation - 2006 Legal Studies.
Barry University : Orlando ,Florida -Bachelor of Liberal studies or Legal studies. -U.S.A. 2009.
New Orleans Baptist Theological Seminary- New Orleans -LA. M.Div. -1992
Nova southeastern University -Orlando, Florida - U.S.A. 2010 -MBA.

EVERGLADES UNIVERSITY- Maitland , FLORIDA -M.B.A. , Executive Master of Business Administration- general Business 2017 , NORTH CENTRAL UNIVERSITY, PH.D.B.A. ,ARIZONA , U.S.A.

Business - 2015-2017 .
Notary public -U.S.A.
Chaplain National and international

www.ingramcontent.com/pod-product-compliance
Lightning Source LLC
Chambersburg PA
CBHW051309120626
46547CB00015B/2157